Pagan Portals

Magick for Empaths

Pagan Portals

Magick for Empaths

Raven Digitalis

London, UK
Washington, DC, USA

First published by Moon Books, 2025
Moon Books is an imprint of Collective Ink Ltd.,
Unit 11, Shepperton House, 89 Shepperton Road, London, N1 3DF
office@collectiveinkbooks.com
www.collectiveinkbooks.com
www.moon-books.net

For distributor details and how to order please visit the 'Ordering' section on our website.

ISBN:978 1 80341 841 4
978 1 80341 937 4 (ebook)
Library of Congress Control Number: 2024945225

A CIP catalogue record for this book is available from the British Library.

Design: Lapiz Digital Services

Cover art: "Equanimity" by Jake Kobrin
Proofreading by Rev. Wendy Branthoover, MFA

UK: Printed and bound by CPI Group (UK) Ltd, Croydon, CR0 4YY
US: Printed and bound by Thomson-Shore, 7300 West Joy Road, Dexter, MI 48130

Contents

Dedicated to all sensitive souls
on life's ever-changing path.
With emotional strength and empathetic grace,
we can and will learn to navigate this place.
Jai Sri Ganesha, Jai Mata Di, Aum Namah Shivaya,
Raven Digitalis

Disclaimer

The information given as part of this book is strictly for educational and entertainment purposes. In absolutely no way is it meant as a substitute for proper medical diagnosis and treatment by registered healthcare professionals. It is very strongly recommended that you consult a licensed healthcare practitioner for any physical or psychological ailments you may have.

Raven Digitalis (USA) is an award-winning author best known for his "empath's trilogy," consisting of *The Empath's Oracle, Esoteric Empathy*, and *The Everyday Empath*, as well as the "shadow trilogy" of *A Gothic Witch's Oracle, A Witch's Shadow Magick Compendium*, and *Goth Craft*. Originally trained in Georgian Witchcraft, Raven has been an earth-based practitioner since 1999, a Priest since 2003, a Freemason since 2012, and an empath all of his life. He holds a degree in cultural anthropology from the University of Montana, jointly operated a nonprofit Pagan temple for sixteen years, and is also a professional Tarot reader, editor, card-carrying magician, and animal rights advocate.

www.ravendigitalis.com

www.facebook.com/ravendigitalis

Photo by Marshall Hibbard

Opening Meditation: Empowering the Empath

To open this guidebook, I would like to offer a chakra meditation with the empathic soul in mind. Most readers will be at least somewhat familiar with the seven primary chakras of the human body. First recognized in ancient Indian Vedic texts, wisdom of the chakras and the body's energy system has now spread far beyond Hinduism and Vedantic philosophy.

Perhaps the best known text referencing the chakra system is the *Yoga Kundali Upanishad*. Wisdom of the chakras is tied with both ancient Indian metaphysics *and* science, and is most deeply explored in Tantric systems of Hindu philosophy. This is primarily evident within various branches of *Shaktism*, all being focused on the Great Goddess (Devi/Durga) in her multitude of forms alongside her multifaceted consort Lord Shiva.

The word *chakra* means "wheel," and refers to the various points on the body where energy accumulates and is processed. These wheel-like vortices, according to traditional Indian medicine (*Ayurveda*), are believed to exist in every person's etheric body, situated along the spinal column, upholding and circulating our *prana* (life energy).

The chakras are said to be "force centers" or whirlpools of energy permeating from points on the body, their energies circulating in an endless fan-shaped formation. Rotating vortices of subtle matter, they are considered the focal points for the reception and transmission of life's experiences. Various systems posit a varying number of chakras, both major and minor, and sometimes recognize chakras situated above and below the physical body. For our purposes we will focus on the primary seven centered along the spine and head.

It is typical for chakras to be depicted as either flower-like or wheel-like. In the former, a specific number of "petals" are shown around the perimeter of a circle. In the latter, a certain number of spokes divide the circle into segments that make the chakra resemble a wheel. Each chakra can be astrally seen as having a specific number of segments or petals. Artistic interpretations of the chakras, both ancient and modern, can be easily researched, as can their numerous alignments to colors, tones, mantras, scents, gemstones, deities, and so much more. Similar to the esoteric Qabalah's attributions of endless alignments with the sephiroth on the Tree of Life, metaphysical associations with the chakras are incredibly expansive. If any of these associations assist you in this meditation, by all means feel free to integrate what you feel called toward.

This meditation is designed especially for those who identify as empaths. We will take a gentle visualization journey through our chakras to see if any unhealthy empathic energy ties or blockages present themselves; these are often formed through experiences related to our past. Chakras are believed to be the points of the body onto which experiential energy may become attached, for better or worse, impacting our overall health. In this meditation we will choose to gently sever any empathetic ties that no longer serve our spiritual functioning. Keep in mind that we don't necessarily need to know the reason for chakra blockages, great or small, but it's important to tend to the energy at hand and analyze it at a later time.

1. Because empathy is specifically aligned with the element Water, this meditation is best performed in a bathtub or body of water. If this is not an option, take a very hot shower and lay down in a comfortable spot where you won't be disturbed. Set the mood with natural incense and even some gentle nonvocal music such as Indian

flutes or ragas. Find yourself duly and truly prepared to journey through your energetic body.

2. Once settled comfortably, declare something along the lines of, "*Great guardians, guides, and invisible helpers, please assist me in journeying my chakras and cleansing imbalances that no longer serve. I come back to center, free from attachment.*" Perform some deep breathing and relax your muscles. You are protected and safe.
3. First chakra: *Muladhara*. Bring your attention to the base of your spine and the erogenous zone of the perineum ("taint"). Visualize this area as a deep swirling red color. This is where energies related to survival are situated. Here we find our base, animalistic instincts and our will to live. Sense blockages in this space and spiral them outward to dissipate, replaced by a deep, healthy, rotating red energy. When it feels comfortably aligned, vocally repeat the mantra "*Lam*" until your intuition tells you to proceed.
4. Second chakra: *Svadhisthana*. Bring your attention just beneath your navel, seeing its swirling and spiraling orange color. This is the area where sexuality resides, and any issues associated with sex. It governs our instincts of nurturing and our own receptivity to nurturing energies. Sense any blockages, willing them to spirally dissipate with the replacement of a strong, bold orange colored energy. When ready, repeat the mantra "*Vam*" out loud until the chakra feels comforted, nurtured, and healthy enough to move on.
5. Third chakra: *Manipura*. Bring your attention to the solar plexus area of the body, beneath the sternum and above the bellybutton. This yellow-colored chakra is where energies of self-confidence and identity are stored. This is the place of ego and self-identity, and is concerned with our

personal place and power in the world. Sense blockages, commanding them to spiral outward to dissipate and be replaced with a strong, radiant yellow. To seal the healing, repeat the mantra "*Ram*" for as long as you see fit.

6. Fourth chakra: *Anahata*. Bring your attention to the heart chakra, located in the sternum and radiating outward in brilliant hues of green. This chakra mediates the three lower and three upper chakras, and is the place from which empaths are most empowered. Overseeing issues of love, compassion, and kindness, pay special attention to blockages in this area, as empaths are prone to hold onto energies that have hurt our hearts. See these energies spiraling outward and onward, replaced by a brilliant swirling green. Invite energies of cosmic, universal, and unconditional love. Repeat the mantra "*Yam*" as much as you see fit before moving on.
7. Fifth chakra: *Vishuddha*. Bring your attention to the throat area, visualizing cycling shades of gorgeous blue. This chakra oversees our "voice" and projection in the world, as well as our boundaries and interpersonal communication. Strongly vocalize the mantra "*Ham*" as swirling blue colors cast off blockages in this area. When feeling empowered, move onward.
8. Sixth chakra: *Ajna*. Bring your attention to the brow; the third-eye center that governs our psychic senses and our perception of reality. This indigo-colored chakra is often seen as the color of a blacklight bulb, and gently swirls in a dance with our mental faculties, encompassing our psychic prowess, dreaming, memory, and mental health in general. Allowing the otherworldly indigo color to heal and send away blockages surrounding perception, repeat the mantra "*Sham*" as many times as you see fit before moving on.

9. Seventh chakra: *Sahasrara*. Bring attention to the crown of your head. This chakra, often seen in hues of violet and otherworldly white, connects us to our higher purpose, to interdimensional planes, and to our greater spiritual wisdom. Blockages here are easily blasted off with powerful white light, swirling in a fashion that connects our individual selves to the journey of our soul. With a smile on your face, repeat the mantra *"Om"* (or *"Aum"*) as many times as you'd like before concluding the meditation.
10. Finalize the meditation by seeing all chakras rotating and blending seamlessly, gently, and powerfully. Visualize your entire body surrounded in comforting white light, all bound together by the healthy light expressions of each chakra. See this light radiating a few feet outside of your body, and finish by taking deep breaths to integrate the energies, knowing that you've given yourself the gift of deeper alignment. See this light as a protective shield, guarding your precious energy centers and thereby all levels of yourself by extension.
11. With your right hand, draw an invisible cross down your body from crown to sternum and shoulder to shoulder, locking in the light. Slowly come back to your body, smile, and – with hands at your heart – give thanks both to the powers that be, and to your beautiful empathic heart. It is a blessing that you exist here and now.

The Elements of Empathy

Hail and welcome to *Magick for Empaths*! We find ourselves here, in this world, in this time, perceiving reality with these bodies and minds. We actively participate in the dance of consciousness, striving every day to meet our needs and, without a doubt, the needs of those around us to the best of our abilities.

Just take a look at ourselves. We are extraordinary. We are instruments of consciousness, transmitting and transmuting energy in every passing moment. Our bodies, and all physical reality, are made up of atoms constantly interacting with and perceiving our environment. Even considering the horrors and chaos of the world, something inside us knows that we're supposed to be here. That we are meant to exercise positive influence to assist the world on a global scale. Every action echoes out and constructs the future unfolding of reality for ourselves, others in the world, and those preparing to enter this plane.

Our senses are alight, and what a blessing they are; they mustn't be taken for granted. We, ourselves, are particularly empathetic. Emotions are our guiding light in the entirety of life's experience. We are emotional beings by nature, and we recognize that emotions take precedence every step of the way. We realize that the mark we make in the world should be one of kindness, gentleness, and positivity. That having been said, let's review what it means to be an empath.

About This Book

This guidebook, part of the *Pagan Portals* series, will explore the ins and outs of the empathic experience and what it means for magickal practitioners. Whether you're a Witch, occultist, mystic, esotericist, or are simply interested in metaphysical perspectives, you're bound to find something here that helps inform your practice.

This little book can be considered an addendum to my previous "empath's triptych" or trilogy, consisting of *Esoteric Empathy, The Everyday Empath,* and *The Empath's Oracle* deck, all printed with Llewellyn Worldwide. Here, I will review some pertinent pieces of information covered in those previous projects, and will introduce quite a bit of new material uniquely for our purposes.

In contrast to my academic and visionary works in the past empathic trilogy, *Magick for Empaths* wanted to be written in a much more engaging and embracing style than anything I've penned in the past. I welcome you with open arms of loving safety.

I have designed (or partially *received*) this book to embrace a bit more intimacy. In other words, I invite you to step a bit more into my world, and meet me in a space of emotional openness. Our time is valuable. Let's make the most of it.

As an aside, I am compelled to mention that no part of this book is the product of Artificial Intelligence. AI plays no part in this or any of my books, and I do say: reader beware when purchasing or listening to modern books, music, and other forms of media. Such strange times we live in.

Gratitude to Moon Books, a division of Collective Ink in London, for printing this guidebook alongside my first-ever fiction project, *Black Magick: 13 Tales of Darkness, Horror & the Occult*. While these particular books were not suitable for my US publishers, I'm grateful to Moon for going out on a limb! My gratitude also extends to each and every reader.

I'm glad you are here.

Empathy in Brief

Empathy is a term that's been gaining traction since its more widespread recognition in the 1960s. At that time in the West, psychology was becoming a more well-rounded scientific field. Emotions were becoming accepted as significant, legitimate, and transformative aspects of the human experience. Countercultures and revolutionary movements were on the rise, striving to break free of suffocating social norms and ingrained constraints, promoting individuality and love above all else.

Media and the arts likewise saw shifts and expansions in subject matter at this time, finally going where no man had gone before. In fact, the term "empath," in reference to someone's innate disposition, was brought into the public eye in 1968's episode of *Star Trek* called "The Empath," featuring a humanoid extraterrestrial who would absorb surrounding emotional energy and transmute others' pain. Later in the series, in 1987, a mainstay "half-empath-half-human" character was introduced as the ship's counselor. In the year 2000 and onward, shows like *Charmed* and *Angel* also made use of the term empath for various characters. It was becoming clear that empath as a self-descriptive term was here to stay in the twenty-first century.

If you're reading these words, odds are you identify as an empath or are curious if the term applies to you personally. First, let it be known that everyone possesses empathic capability to one degree or another, much as we do with psychic abilities. In fact, my favorite definition of the term is "emotional psychic."

It's important to note that empathy cannot be reduced to mere "emotional sensitivity." Highly sensitive people are not necessarily empaths, but all empaths are highly sensitive people. To simply be emotional is not the mark of an empath.

Everyone is empathic to one degree or another. Some, like ourselves, are more empathic than the majority. We highly empathic folks are, ideally, helping guide others to becoming more emotionally caring. We can't force this, but we can most definitely lead by example!

Because the term empath is being used (and misused) tremendously in modern spiritual circles, we need to recognize it for what it is. Word to the wise: if someone in the metaphysical field says that they are *not* particularly empathetic, and are more prone to, say, psychic or mediumistic work, *believe them*, because they have the self-awareness to state such a fact!

Those of us who demonstrate high levels of emotional absorption tend to mirror other people, usually unconsciously. *Emotional contagion*, catching others' emotions, is very much part of how humans and other animals operate socially, and has been shown to be an evolutionary trait. When socially interacting with others, we are prone to mimic other people's mannerisms, expressions, and even accents. We are not play-pretending; instead, it's a natural response. Cooperation is our natural state.

Empathy is recognized in scientific circles to be a characteristic that aids in the evolution of a species. Evolutionary success is possible because we are programmed to help each other. Unnecessary conflict is our bane, and is also why we tend to be people-pleasers.

Some fields of study cite *mirror neurons*: areas in the animalistic brain that prompt us to unconsciously mimic our surroundings. Although this piece of physiological research is currently under greater study, we do indeed, on a psychological level, tend to unconsciously mimic expressions portrayed by those surrounding us. This is human nature. We can see this with the universal experience of yawning. If someone yawns, human or animal, most of us will yawn in return. This is how we're wired.

A massively important piece of the puzzle is that true empathy involves compassion, not just emotional absorption or physiological mimicry. Empathy is a genuine, responsive care for others, whether human, animal, or environmental. That's just it. We cannot confuse it for anything else: genuine empathy embodies emotional care and compassion.

Empathy bonds us all together; it unites us as a species and as navigators of life's experience. Empathy is not without its challenges and pitfalls, which I'll examine shortly and throughout. Compassion to a fault is a very real and detrimental thing.

Emotions are a strength, not a weakness. Emotions are our guide. The strongest among us, as many ancients would attest, both recognize and seek to resolve our emotional states at any given time. Emotions are part of the gift of life; don't believe silly modern social conditioning that tells us to toughen up and bottle everything down.

Conditioning through generations is slowly being broken in society at large. Like a pendulum that has been frozen at one extreme and is finally freed, it takes time to achieve a moderation of balance. In the meantime, individual conscious awareness is necessary in bringing that greater societal balance to fruition sooner rather than later.

We must be realistic with ourselves, as well as when interacting with those around us. We can't believe everything we think, and we can't affirm everyone else in whatever they themselves are thinking. Emotions come and go, and it usually takes a bit of stepping-back to determine their source and validity.

Empaths, and those who are prone to intense empathetic experiences, are naturally introspective. That's our disposition. Although we can have moments of extroversion when we're feeling especially confident in social situations, we tend to default to an introspective and introvertive baseline.

Empathic capabilities wax and wane throughout the day and throughout life in general, but everyone has an emotional baseline, just as one has a baseline regarding psychic abilities, mediumship abilities, and other skills of perception, cognition, and processing. Those who consider themselves empaths are individuals who exhibit a higher-than-average amount of empathy on a regular basis. We have the distinct responsibility of self-awareness if we want to keep these beautiful gifts in check. It's a disadvantage to confuse others' emotions for our own!

Empaths have the ability to relate to a wide variety of people and perspectives, and are often understood to be trustworthy, even by total strangers. We are guided by emotion, and will make choices in life based on feelings and intuition. We are generally warm and mild-mannered, particularly valuing beauty, gentleness, and innocence. We feel safe with animals, and often with children, knowing that they don't have dangerous ulterior motives.

Empaths are drawn toward all things mystical, and are artists by nature. We have an innate desire to help alleviate suffering and to help make the world a better place however we can. We are generally considerate, thoughtful, and generous (sometimes to a fault), but it's not because we're looking for something in return. We know deep down that everything in life is interconnected and interdependent, and we know that our mission is to help uplift, not tear down.

Empathy is strictly emotional, full stop. Although some New Age flights of fancy would have one believe that there are different "types" of empaths, there is only one at the end of the day: emotional empaths. Empathy is necessarily bound to the emotional experience and, while every highly empathic person has additional talents and proclivities, the empathic experience doesn't need to be superimposed on these callings For example, a person is not a "crystal empath," but rather "an empath who is talented in working with gemstones."

Another term to make note of is "dark empath," which refers to someone who exhibits what appear to be empathetic characteristics, but who is actually trying to gain the trust of others in a manipulatory way. These types will intentionally gather knowledge of emotional vulnerabilities and hold them as future ammunition in a psychological arsenal.

This is not actually empathy; it's a form of narcissism and narcissistic abuse. These individuals may have the *cognition* to understand someone's emotions, but it doesn't mean they care. There is a disconnect. Someone who is exercising *sympathy* responds compassionately without necessarily stepping into the other's emotional experience, but those who feign empathy, so-called "dark empaths," only care about others if it directly affects themselves. This self-centeredness and lack of care are textbook characteristics of narcissistic personality disorder. These individuals are experts at pretending to care, at making others feel heard. But, at the end of the day, it comes back to their desire to gain power, control, and emotional leverage over the empath.

As I mentioned, true empathy is characterized by not only absorbing the emotions of others we're interacting with or observing, but incorporates a response of compassion. Empaths feel, sense, and absorb emotion, and also exhibit a response of genuine care.

This is why the ill-equated term "dark empathy" is not empathy at all; it is self-serving manipulation beneath a façade of care. Unregulated empaths are easy targets; we can easy fall prey to individuals prone to narcissism and sociopathic tendencies. If you suspect you may be the victim of this, please look up *apathy, antipathy,* and the term *alexithymia,* and research the work of the brilliant Dr. Ramani Durvasula on YouTube. Sometimes we don't even see these things coming, particularly if we struggle with self-confidence. It is our responsibility to know ourselves and to look out for our own best interests rather than getting swept away in human drama and deceit. The psychological trauma that results from the empath-narcissist relationship is brutal. Getting away from the situation is essential because it is abusive. Therapy is huge in healing the damage, as not all of us are equipped with the tools to do this independently. Prevention is the best medicine.

Because our natures are (when we are at baseline) kind and genuine, we assume that everyone else must function similarly. It can be depressing and disillusioning when an empath learns that not everyone has each other's best interest in mind. We must keep protected and aware, realizing that we can help inspire empathy in others but don't have the responsibility of forcing those less empathetic to grow a bigger heart.

The empathic experience is beautiful, powerful, and deeply needed in all aspects of life and all across the world. But, of course, being highly empathic comes with its own unique set of obstacles and shortcomings. It's all about finding balance.

Empathic Challenges & Mindfulness

Occurrences of emotional overload make the empathic ability feel like a curse or disability. In truth, it's quite the opposite. It would be both folly and irresponsible of me to say that there is nothing wrong with you as an empath. We are not perfect beings. Our challenges in daily life are very real. When empaths are stressed, imbalanced, and utterly overwhelmed with the experience of reality, we are anything but perfect.

Sometimes we turn to overusing drink, drugs, junk food, social media, gaming, sex, and other dependencies that help us feel a bit more temporarily capable of dealing with the world at large. These are distractions from how we are feeling, and are ultimately destructive to our well-being. Self-care is essential to minimizing the need for distraction or emotional anesthetization. This is not something to be ashamed of, but we need to recognize that due to our deeply emotional disposition, our minds may seek outlets for coping with intense internal experiences.

We *feel* the experience of life more deeply than most people do. And to think how this has played out in our history, not only with the incomprehensible Witch hunts in the West (and further), but with modern warfare and social injustices, we find ourselves alienated from and vulnerable to the world at large. This is a scary place, but it is also a necessary place for us to be at this time, or else we wouldn't be here.

Only we can become our own best friend and advocate. As much as we can rely on others to help guide the way, this book included, we are the ones that must fight for ourselves and decide to be the primary proponents for our physical, mental, emotional, and spiritual health. There is no one to save us but ourselves, and we are capable.

Because we experience life from a platform of emotional sensitivity, when our wellbeing is sabotaged we often default to one of two reactions: people-pleasing or shutting down.

The people-pleasing response is one of striving to avoid all conflict entirely, while emotionally shutting down is a response of self-preservation. Many empaths are prone to anxiety, and its bedfellow, depression, because our experiences in life can leave us feeling overwhelmed and uncertain how to respond.

Many of us are neurodivergent or "neurospicy," which is simply another disposition to navigate. We empaths have so much in common and also incredible uniqueness from one person to the next. Our individuality makes us who we are, so operating within our neurological, social, and psychological dispositions offers us each a special angle for operating in life.

The idea of normal, or normality, is fictional. All of us experience reality from a different vantage point, which many mystics perceive as the Universe experiencing itself. We can ascribe "God" or "gods" to this understanding, but it's all the same: *we are consciousness perceiving and interacting with itself.*

As deeply emotional beings, ascribing and describing ourselves as empaths, we hold a special place in this current experience of reality. Feelings of hopelessness can convince us that we have nothing to offer in the world. That we are raw emotional nerves experiencing life at the whim of whomever may surround us at any given time. But it's not true. We can't believe our inner critic all the time, as much as it's there to protect us. Many of our insecurities are rooted in social conditioning and the experiences we've lived to this point. However, we are not defined by our past.

We view ourselves and reality through a lens we have been conditioned to understand through experience. Using the now-world-renowned practice of mindfulness – stepping back from ourselves to view a greater picture – we can more accurately perceive not only ourselves but also other people and the world at large. When we become more mindful, we become less judgmental of ourselves and reality as a whole. It doesn't take much.

Please pay attention. It's time to step back from this book, and step into yourself.

Become aware of yourself in this present moment. Just do it. Please. You're reading these words... first step! You recognize that I typed these words in a different time from when you're reading them. Check. You are aware of yourself in the present moment: your eyes open, your body sensing the world around you.

Smell through your nose; what is it like? It's likely neutral. Hear the environment around you, whatever it is. Simply become aware of it, don't judge it. Use your sensory faculties to become aware of the present moment.

You are reading or listening to this guidebook in the present moment. Take some deep breaths, slowly – nasal breathing is key – and feel yourself aware, here, now.

Bring to mind the most challenging thing or things in your reality at this present time. Look at them like you are watching someone else engage in this charade of emotional tug-of-war. You have been through some tough times, and so have we all.

Just take a breath. *You are not your emotions.* You are a magickal empath, and your truest nature is one of loving kindness.

You don't have to dive too deep right now. Simply become aware of your thoughts, emotions, and reflections at this time. As they come up, send them Universal Light. Breathe deeply through your nose and out of your mouth, sending loving light to whatever challenges come up in your mind.

Now, bring your focus back to your body and your physical senses. Come out with a deeper awareness of which challenges your life is offering you at this point. Write it down and make a list if you'd like. Feel free to perform the shadow work meditation at the end of this book now if you feel guided to, or wait until later.

You are the magick. Perform whatever sending-offs of light that means in the present moment, whether it's lighting a candle and incense toward traumas of the past, or simply inhaling cosmic light to assist in guiding your future. Whatever you have experienced in the past, you are here now in the present moment and are forging the future by *your own commandment.* You are in charge of your life. You are beautiful.

Perhaps the greatest problem we empaths face is that of protection: protecting ourselves from external vibrations that are unsavory, unkind, or otherwise negative. This is why we have a tendency to isolate and cultivate our social situations with utmost care – whenever possible, at least. Later I will explore techniques for working with the necessity for social and energetic protection, but for now let's look at some of our hangups and how they relate to self-regulation and awareness.

I'll be the first to say that highly empathic persons struggle to understand sarcasm, and damn can we be gullible. We are not the first to understand social cues, as we expect everyone else to be as forthright as we are. We operate from an emotional platform and sometimes forget that not everyone does the same.

When overwhelmed in public situations, anxiety, fatigue, and migraines commonly ensue. Groups and social situations can be utterly overwhelming. But we can most certainly navigate this with magickal and metaphysical practice, which I will soon get into.

As a general rule, empaths have trouble distinguishing our own emotions from those of other people. We get wrapped up in social dramas because we want to help, even if it's actually none of our business. Much of the time we are indeed able to assist others in need, even by providing a listening ear and kind reassurance, but at other times we may accidentally enable poor behavior by trying to keep the peace. This is why it's important to take a step back to think things through, whether regarding our own actions and responses or observing other people's.

We must extend the same care for ourselves that we would do for others. We can achieve balance by having healthy daily routines, with therapy, medication (naturopathic or allopathic), meditation, spiritual practice, and numerous other methodologies. Everyone is different and responds differently to modalities of wellness. Sometimes it's best to take personal space for a little bit, get some rest and nutrients, and remember that feelings of depression and anxiety will pass. (Although if the depression and anxiety are chronic and ongoing, professional help is the greatest option – we're all in it together.) The more dedicated we are to discovering and maintaining holistic balance, the greater empathic influence we can exercise in the world.

There are plenty of challenges that come with having a strong empathic capacity. (And there are also plenty more associated with *not* being particularly empathetic!) One of the biggest challenges is empathetic shortsightedness when it comes to social interactions. Because we are naturally focused on the exchange of emotional energy at any given time, it can be difficult to keep track of what someone is verbally communicating; it takes practice to maintain balance in society.

I would like to review some common empathic struggles using myself as an example. My point in reciting some personal experiences is to help readers identify with the energetic exchanges in each situation, pinpointing how I was empathically shortsighted. I hope these examples can help you better understand experiences you may have undergone in your own life or may experience in future. These stories reflect an empath's common struggle of perceiving the greater picture in any given moment.

- As a young teenage Witch, I befriended a girl who claimed to have an impressive lineage of occult training and an abundance of supernatural power. She also claimed to be a sanguine vampire, having numerous underground vampiric friends around town that I was not privy to meet. She claimed to have spirit guides of every imaginable variety, and boasted a plethora of mysterious lineages and initiations. Young and wide-eyed, I had no reason to doubt her. We would go on paranormal adventures in cemeteries, abandoned buildings, and empty fields; these visitations were always invigorating because she would perceive and react to loads of astral entities that I simply was unable to see. If a breeze suddenly picked up or the rain began to fall, she would casually mention that it was she who had influenced the weather to shift. For a couple years I went along with what she said, mostly in stride and with curiosity, until later realizing – by others pointing it out – that she was in fact a pathological liar. This had never occurred to me, and is a similar style of manipulation that cult leaders utilize to take advantage of impressionable seekers. Empaths tend to have difficulty understanding when others are being disingenuous, so we must strive for discernment as much as humanly possible!

- Once upon a time in India, I was purchasing samosas and sweets at a street stall, when someone came up to me and others asking for rupees. This person was clearly a *hijra*: a member of India's ancient third-gendered community. These folks are generally born males who have undergone castration; they are believed to have the power to bless or curse, which is why they are hired for wedding festivals, births, spiritual rites of passage, and other celebrations of life. When she came up to me and others, I was giggling because of the language barrier. For the life of me I couldn't figure out why she was asking for money, but I eventually surrendered 100 rupees because the store clerk (who spoke both Hindi and English) said that I should. It was only later that my anthropological training came back into mind: hijras should *always* be given monetary offerings to ensure future blessings. I knew this well and had even written about it in my first book! In the moment, however, all of my schooling had gone out of the window because I was solely focused on trying to make sense of the emotional energetic exchange, neglecting basic cognition and the art of memory!
- I once became an unwitting participant in a complex scam. My friend in an African country, with whom I had developed a trusted relationship (and still have), came asking for assistance: a friend of his needed the down payment for his first apartment in order to get off the streets. All I had to do was be the middleman: receive $1100 USD on Venmo from a woman in the US; she was

his friend's friend. I was the only one in the scenario who had the ability to transform the Venmo money into Bitcoin and send it on Cash App, which I was able and willing to do. I received the Venmo money, did the Bitcoin transfer, and felt good about lending a hand. The following week, I received a notice that my Venmo account was frozen due to a complaint from the American woman. It turned out that my African friend's "friend" was actually only someone he had recently "met" on Instagram. He had been pulling the wool over not only my friend's eyes, but also this generous woman's eyes simultaneously. He ghosted them both upon receiving my transfer. The financial liability, due to her rightful complaint, fell on my shoulders, as I could not prove what had happened. It took some time to pay off the fine and get my account back in good standing. It's incredible how complex virtual scams are becoming, and the lengths to which one will "play" others by forming intricate stories that pull at their heartstrings. Empaths beware!

- When living in Hawaii, I had concluded an afternoon of enjoying a large weekly drumming and dancing circle. As the sun began to set, I made friends with a couple of fellow attendees and, once it got dark, everyone besides us were cleared out of the public park. I offered a ride to a new acquaintance, a Hawaiian-born fellow with Japanese lineage. It turned out that my vehicle (the only one remaining) was surrounded by a group of young Hawaiian locals. They, like many locals, did not like nor understand my appearance: tall and Gothic with loads of ear piercings, a bindi, and visible eyeliner. The "leader" demanded to know, "*what* are you?" to which I excitedly responded "I'm a Witch!" This was not the correct answer. Harassment and heckling ensued. One of the girls in the group eventually took me aside and explained that the word I used means something different there, and I just need to leave immediately. This was something I was already very much well aware of in theory; just apparently not in practice. If it wasn't for my new local acquaintance talking the group down from an enraged state, I'm quite sure I would have been either roughed up or "disappeared" that night; an occurrence that happens far too often in Hawaii, especially to non-Islanders. Again, all of my anthropological training had gone out the window and I was only able to see my communicative mistake in hindsight. It's wise to remember that we *are* capable of modifying our words and verbiage depending on the situation!

- Shortly after relocating to Hawaii, where I resided for a few years for a fresh start, I met a buddy online through an online dating site. He and I had spent time some together here and there, and we decided we were best suited as friends. One afternoon, I drove to the road located down from his house to pick him up for a day on the beach. I pulled over on the side of the road to text and wait; it turned out he was unable to make it. Just then, a large landscaping truck and trailer pulled behind my car, fully blocking me in. A local man came out screaming, threatening to use his gun. Why? Because it turned out I was parked in his driveway. I was terrified and frozen, explaining from inside my vehicle that I didn't realize it was a driveway; I thought it was a pull-off. It turns out his daughter was inside and called him from work because she thought someone was scouting the house. It was only then that I realized the area I was parked led to a house at the bottom of a hill. Despite numerous apologies, his tirade of threats and insults continued for a good ten minutes. I was too scared in the moment to realize that I should have phoned my other friends or the police, all of whom were located less than two blocks away. Instead, the emotional exchange was overwhelming and, by focusing on the immediate exchange alone, I was further putting myself in danger and not seeing the forest for the trees: help was nearby and I was too shocked to recount that fact. He eventually let me leave, but not before taking photos of me, my car, and even my driver's license – he was going to break the window and grab it if I refused to hand it over. He swiftly spread the word around town about the new creepy Mainlander in town. Luckily, most others in Hawaii demonstrated great Aloha spirit, but the handful who didn't certainly made up for it!

- For more years than I care to count, I was mistreated by someone I explicitly trusted spiritually and entirely. My life was intertwined with them and, despite warnings by countless others, I was unable to see or admit the extent of increasing mistreatment. I would make every excuse in the book for them, refusing to admit that this person was in fact corrupt. Although I don't regret that period in my life, I realize now in hindsight that this person was taking advantage of me for everything I had: everything from finances to time to emotional dependency. It took a few major incidents, and a fever-pitch brush with suicidal ideation, to realize that I had to remove myself from their influence. This meant entirely upending my life, moving to Hawaii, experiencing years of grieving, and eventually picking myself back up from the ashes of narcissistic abuse. Two of the hardest empathic lessons I learned from this were to *not* feel required to forgive the person, and to *not* merely wish them "the best." The latter, which my Witch Godmother Deb McGaw taught me, is because some people's idea of "best" involves deeply manipulating others for personal gain. Instead,

> I wish them awareness. That's the best we can wish for ourselves and for all.

I hope these examples can provide readers with some idea of the dangers we face when we don't activate our intelligent minds in the midst of emotional social exchanges. It's all too easy to focus on how everyone is feeling rather than what they're saying or doing. We empaths are prone to not seeing the greater picture and to neglecting our cognitive intelligence in social situations.

This leaves us vulnerable to harsh experiences, sometimes putting us in very real danger. This empathic shortsightedness can occur in any given moment or stretched over a course of time. We can better navigate social life by taking a step back *mentally and mindfully* at any given time in order to witness our happenings with greater clarity.

Balancing Mind & Heart

Our thoughts and emotions are projections of our spirit, our consciousness awareness, and we are greatly defined by both. Thoughts and emotions constantly interplay, each affecting the other. This helps us function as human animals in the world, but can also be detrimental when uncontrolled. It's essential, especially as empaths, and even more especially as magickal empaths, to exercise emotional control and awareness of our thoughts as much as possible at any given time.

Regardless of how we discovered magickal spirituality, we find our hearts beating to the rhythm of nature. We also find that the natural world is reflected within us, through the cycles and stages of development of our bodies and minds. Like our plant and animal comrades, we are part of the natural world. Yet unlike plants and other animals, our thoughts and emotions tend to be particularly complex. Nonhuman animals also exhibit instincts, feelings, and emotions, but what sets us humans apart is our level of attachment to our experiences. We emotionally and cognitively process life differently than other animals; there's no denying it! While we do indeed function like other animals on base levels, including biological instincts and basic feelings, humans are a distinctly complex species of overthinkers and overfeelers.

Because our thoughts and emotions are experiential, rattling off categorical descriptions of these here and now would not do the subjects justice. In fact, numerous philosophers and theorists catalog the spectrums of human emotion and cognition in a multitude of ways – sometimes *vastly* different ways! However we choose to define them, our thoughts and emotions require recognition, responsibility, and awareness. If we *own* our thoughts and our emotions, we own our magick.

Spellcasting, meditation, and prayer operate on both interior and exterior levels. Intentional focus on such things, and on life itself, resonate both cosmically (esoterically) and psychologically (mentally). The famed Hermetic axiom "as above, so below" may also be applied to the saying, "as within, so without." Because of this connection with the micro (Self) and macro (Universe), the ways in which we conduct our thoughts and our emotional responses has an effect both on our daily perspectives and on the global spiritual landscape. Thoughts, we find, are often directly linked to our emotional responses. For this reason, a magickal practitioner has a unique responsibility of exercising emotional awareness and mental precision, whether it's in daily life or during a formal ritualistic undertaking.

We humans, Witchy or otherwise, are creatures of feeling. Emotions enrich our experience of life, deeply influencing our daily modes of thought and, for us, our regular magickal work. Aside from individuals who may suffer a medical condition that directly relates to affective functioning, the great majority of individuals have access to the full, beautiful spectrum of human emotions. It's simply a matter of what we are tapped into at any given moment.

Witches, Pagans, and mystics regularly practice "seeing through the veil," which also ideally applies to our *own* veil! The mind can play tricks at times. Emotions can feel all-pervasive if we don't take a step back and become an observer… this is why Buddhism and other Eastern spiritual paths maintain a constant focus on mindfulness and present-moment awareness. They've got a point! I will explore this more in depth later on.

Everyone is psychologically wired differently from birth and from experience (and undoubtedly from previous lifetimes), which is why no emotional issue ever has a single solution or remedy; it's not one-size-fits-all. Everyone connects with emotions in a unique manner. Emotions and emotional responses are a personal thing. Everyone has different emotional strengths and hindrances.

Emotions can feel fragile, it's true, but we are powerful beings. As dedicated esotericists, we must strive to be honest with ourselves as much as we possibly can. This includes emotional honesty. No one can be expected to function at 100% self-awareness 24/7, but if we can regularly keep our emotional tides in check, we soon find that life's ups, downs, twists, and turns don't have to overtake us every time. Empaths are sensitive, and our sensitivities can be incredible boons in the journey of life. If we seek to be as balanced as possible in our thoughts and emotions, as well as in our responses and reactions, we can encourage similar awareness in others and lead by example.

While it might be easier said than done at times, positive thinking really is a key to our survival – not to mention our esoteric success. If we can train our minds to default to optimism rather than pessimism, we find that the world is still a marvelously, breathtakingly beautiful place despite its dreadful challenges.

Choosing to think positively doesn't imply that we should put on happy masks or pretend that we're fine even when we're not. We are many things, but "fake" is not one of them. We can acknowledge our own troubles – and the abject horrors of the world – while simultaneously choosing to shift our mental focus to lighter and less somber states of perception to the best of our abilities.

Conscious redirection requires *humility*: one of the most valuable spiritual assets we can invoke. By remaining humble we can more easily learn from mistakes and exercise forgiveness for ourselves and for others. Through humility we can gracefully step back from mental and emotional clutter in order to redirect ourselves in a more spiritually conscious manner.

It takes practice to invoke regular positive thinking into one's daily routine. We need to exercise consistent self-awareness so that we can make the spiritual choice to reroute our mind's reactions as necessary. Keeping good humor and lightheartedness even at the worst of times can go a long way in helping ourselves and helping others in their lives. For example, we are capable of simultaneously feeling both sadness and hope.

Just like pessimism, optimism is contagious. As Witches and occultists, it's our duty to be constantly aware of our effect on the world and the people with whom we interact. The more we work on our own thoughts and modes of communication, we can help turn the world in a slightly more positive direction, bit by bit, day by day, moment by moment – and that's some *very* powerful work!

Because thought is linked with intention, we find that magickal energy follows the flow of our thoughts. Thinking about something invokes its presence on some level; it's simply a matter of what we *do* with those thoughts. As a general rule of perspective, fearful thoughts attract a fearful experience.

Loving thoughts attract a loving experience. In many ways, we magickal folk get to choose our experiences by intentionally directing our subtle energies on a daily basis. Thoughts are linked with emotion, which is majorly relevant to highly empathic folks, and we find that emotions guide our everyday life and our magickal activities.

In a sense, spellcasting occurs every day on a constant basis. *Everyone* actively co-creates reality whether they realize it or not. Spells, prayers, and intentional magick are not limited to occult ritual. Ritualistic procedures can be fulfilling, potent, and transformational, but I heavily argue that the most important ritual we perform is our day-to-day experience. For this reason, we must follow our thoughts and the emotions they have inspired.

I tend to think of spellcasting, prayer, meditation, and ritualized intentions as "peaks," if you will, of our ordinary trains of thought. This is touched on in the final section of this guidebook. We often find ourselves preparing for hours, days, weeks, months, or even years for a specific ritual whose vibration launches into the fabric of the Universe at a designated time. This eventually peaks in what's termed in Wicca as a Cone of Power.

When it comes to intentional magickal procedure, whether group or solitary, we practitioners take some amount of time to plan our activities, ritualize them through action, and conclude by winding down, cleaning up, journaling, and otherwise reminiscing about the experience. In this way, the process of intentional magick can be likened to a mountainous climb, including the ascent (preparation), goal (ritual), and the descent (decompression). Even though our time spent at the mountain's peak may feel timeless and mystical, the whole process was originally created through a process of routine thinking: our everyday minds.

Because our daily thoughts and actions are directly linked to our emotional responses, having acute awareness of our emotional reactions will allow us to trace our thought patterns and distinguish illusion from objective understanding.

Our thoughts influence our emotions and our emotions influence our thoughts. In an effort to gain emotional awareness, we can begin by actively choosing to focus on *how* we think. An easy way to do this is to regularly take a step back and reconsider how we perceive life, including ourselves, in any given moment.

Successful spellcraft is greatly accomplished by way of emotional energy – a fact that is especially pertinent to empaths. We are the absolute and essential component to any given spell or ceremony. We are better able to influence reality through intentional emotional projection than we are from simply "thinking" a spell or going through the motions or recipes without emotional involvement.

Drinking a single drop of rosemary tea with the focused, emotional intention of healing and protection is miles more effective than drinking a whole gallon of the stuff without any emotional focus behind it.

Have you ever heard that old saying, "cast a spell and then forget about it?" The concept seems clear enough: weave your magick into the Universe and then stop feeding it mental energy. The reasoning behind this idea is simple: if you forget about your magick, you leave it in the hands of the gods and spirits and what-have-you. In theory, this ensures that the magician won't agitate or nitpick the energy that has already been projected; it's been put out there and doesn't need to be influenced any further. The mere idea of "forgetting" about a spell implies that a person's everyday thoughts can have an adverse effect on the already-cast spell. I believe that most practitioners would agree with this perspective. But at the same time, does "forgetting" about a spell really work as well in practice?

If I cast a spell of emotional healing for a friend of mine, I could never bring myself to altogether forget about it. Instead, I'm going to check in with my friend regularly and do some follow-up work; that sort of thing is not something that's easily forgotten. If I cast a spell to banish my own pessimism, I'm most certainly going to keep my perspectives in check on a regular basis. If I cast a spell for love, I'm not going to allow myself to live in a perpetual state of fear or hopelessness every day; I'm going to trust myself, trust the Universe, and trust my magick, and will strive to match that loving vibration in my day-to-day.

To try to *entirely* forget about a spell is to be dishonest and, quite frankly, can impede our magickal work. Follow through is part of the magick. This is where occult responsibility comes into play. We must be consistently honest with our thoughts and emotions, understanding the effects our daily perspectives have on our lives. To completely forget about a spell is to pretend like it never happened, and this is dangerous territory both emotionally and psychologically.

A practitioner's thoughts and emotions can either reinforce or unravel their magick. That's a huge thing! We can be our own best magickal cheerleader or our own worst enemy. As thoughts and emotions interplay in our daily lives, we can choose to have them reinforce our magickal and spiritual work or we can choose to have them undo it. Truly, it is not something to be taken lightly. If we actively channel our daily thoughts and emotions concerning our magick, we can add a boost of daily power to spells and rituals that have been performed – this is why we see things like seven-day candles in traditions like hoodoo. Daily reinforcement goes a long way. If we want to empower our magickal work, we need to channel our thoughts and emotions as they arise, whether or not they are attached to our "active" magickal work. As many readers are aware, magick is not about *doing* but about *being*.

Life can be tricky and is sometimes dreadfully difficult. It's easy to become emotionally overwhelmed to the point of hopelessness, but many of the tormenting thoughts inspiring these emotional states are illusory. It can be challenging to work ourselves out of a state of emotional overload or empathic burnout, but where there's a will there's a way. Sometimes this means making lifestyle modifications and working more diligently with techniques of self-awareness in order to craft positive thinking as a steadfast *modus operandi* in daily life. The following are a few options to consider on your own journey of cognitive and emotional wellbeing.

- **Counseling**: I believe that *everyone* deserves counseling and therapy from time to time. Even therapists have therapists. When life is just too overwhelming, individuals who are professionally trained in the workings of the mind can be of great assistance. There are many different styles of counseling, therapy, and life coaching to choose from. Many professionals have online biographies that can help seekers get a better idea for their counseling styles, specialties, and personal values. Free, discount, and sliding-scale therapists are available in many locations. Please keep a list, in your phone or wallet, of crisis hotlines and text-lines for your local area and in your country; these numbers can be discovered with a quick online search, and may assist you or others in immediate need further down the line. The folks at the other end of these hotlines and text-lines are happy to help, are equipped to do so, and are renowned for being greatly helpful in times of need. Additionally, should your or someone else's crisis be life-threatening or otherwise urgent, please don't hesitate to utilize local emergency room services.

- **Journaling & Art**: Possibly one of the most underrated psychological activities, keeping a journal or diary can greatly assist in getting thoughts and emotions "out there." By expressing our thoughts and emotions in a private manner, the energy becomes externalized so it doesn't have to run amuck in our heads. Similarly, artistic expression of any type serves to creatively channel our internal landscape. Not to mention, both journaling and art can be powerfully transformational acts of magickal intention.
- **Medicine**: Although it might be obvious, I should note that *none of the advice herein is a substitute for medical advice*. For many emotionally sensitive individuals, a combination of medication and lifestyle changes can produce dramatic healing effects. This category of "medicine" is not limited to allopathic pharmaceuticals; many people find naturopathic and herbal medicine, or a combination of the two, extremely effective. Everybody has a different constitution so there is no "right" medicinal answer for everyone. If you feel that it may benefit your daily life, I encourage you to speak with a physician and other healthcare professionals to determine if medicine would aid in your own mental and emotional balance.
- **Mindfulness**: A term frequently used in both Buddhism and psychological circles, mindfulness implies self-awareness. To become mindful is to take a step back from our thoughts and emotions in order gain greater psychological equilibrium; in this way, we can take a moment to *detach* from our mind and emotions without actually *disconnecting*. I will explore this theme throughout this guidebook. Mindfulness encompasses the idea of present-moment awareness: to focus on the events of the now rather than stress surrounding the

past or the future. If we can train ourselves to *observe* our thoughts and emotions as frequently as possible, we can more easily take a step back at any given moment. We are not our thoughts. We are not our emotions. These are components that help create this thing we call "self," and with the aid of daily mindfulness we can take a step back and choose to be the ones in control.

- **Ritual**: Who doesn't love a good ritual? Solid ceremonial standards like the Lesser Banishing Ritual of the Pentagram can balance our cognitive and emotional bodies while simultaneously invoking the spiritual realm. Even a powerful recitation of the "Witches' Rune", "Wiccan Rede", the "Desiderata", or uplifting poetic pieces can have instant calming effects. As an empath, when creating your own ceremony, consider incorporating visualizations focused on dumping excessively accumulated energies into the earth. Similarly, it's wise to practice grounding by performing visualizations such as tree rooting.
- **Sleep, Diet & Exercise**: One cannot underestimate the power of good sleep, regular exercise, and a healthy diet of whole, organic, unprocessed foods – and occasional French fries, of course. Our bodies are the divine temples that our spirits have the pleasure of incarnating for this instant in time. Taking care of the body is tending to the soul. It may take time to discover your unique needs and preferences in all of these realms, but the mind and emotions can greatly shift toward the positive once a personal balance is realized and diligently followed.
- **Yoga & Meditation**: Highly advocated in Eastern spiritual traditions, yoga and meditation have profound benefits psychologically, emotionally, physically, and spiritually. There are numerous styles, schools, and philosophies of both yoga and meditation; the two practices are inextricably interlinked. Integrating any

measure of these practices on a regular basis can help emotionally and mentally balance any spiritual seeker. Taking care of the body is essential; it's the only thing we have for the duration. The more we abuse it in youth, the more we pay for it later in life, so let's get on it while we can! While yoga and meditation can seem intimidating to a newcomer, they are much easier to practice than is commonly believed. In many ways, these practices are inherently wired into our brains and bodies; it's just a matter of learning the techniques. It's no wonder that the various styles of yoga and meditation have been practiced since time immemorial, and will most certainly continue to be practiced until our very end.

The Magick of Empathy

Although a deeply social and physiological phenomenon, empathy is most certainly a spiritual force. Magick and nature are intertwined, and empathy is part of our human experience; it's the part of us that invites the world to engage with us in an evolutionary trajectory of compassion and understanding.

Terms like "empathic magick" and "empathic healing" are not standalone practices or methodologies. Instead, the terms refer to empathy as the force that informs any given activity. A successful psychotherapist, for example, utilizes empathy so that they might step into their client's or patient's experience, thereby allowing them to provide the best objective advice possible for that individual. This therapist would not be strictly considered an "empathic healer," but a professional who utilizes the empathic experience for successful therapeutic work.

The same can be said for Witches, Pagans, mystics, and occultists. We have the opportunity to integrate empathy within virtually all of our spiritual work and our lives in general; this is especially the case if empathic sensitivity is our natural proclivity.

The most pivotal magickal work we can do as empaths begins with ourselves. Empathy is a social experience of emotional exchange, and that's something that makes our magickal work a bit more special by necessity. The exchanges we have with others every day is of great importance, especially the manners in which we react and respond to life's experiences. Our very interaction with other people, as well as with our *own* thoughts and emotions, are of utmost importance. Emotional balance is the goal, and gods know we don't get it right all the time.

We can and should take steps to understand and resolve traumatic imprints. We need to become our own advocates.

Inner work is of utmost importance for empaths because we are primarily guided by our emotions. It's from a platform of emotion that we interact with life, with ourselves, and with the magick we weave into reality.

We are extremely powerful individuals, and we deserve to achieve a state of emotional equilibrium. When we are balanced, our magickal work is invigorating and wise.

When approaching magickal aspects of empathy, I find it best to explore it from a lens of modern Western Paganism and Witchcraft. The reason is that it can be difficult to get into the nuances of ceremonial magick in conjunction with the empathic experience. It's within ceremonial or high magickal practices that we find esoteric workings the most formulaic, the magician acting as an instrument for both conducting and instructing terrestrial, cosmic, and interdimensional forces. We see this approach in many rituals of the Golden Dawn and Thelema, as well as in workings Solomonic and Enochian in nature, alongside those of various other Lodge-based esoteric systems.

While the ceremonial approach can very much be successful, potent, and transformative, it doesn't always work for folks who are highly empathic. We tend to be more intuitive in nature, while high magick tends to benefit by having emotions take a backseat to ensure ritual safety and success. Although it's possible for the trained empath to temporarily turn off emotional hypersensitivity, we find ourselves most at home with rituals that utilize emotional depth and connection. We are *all* about feelings, and tend to engage with life's mysteries from an emotional standpoint. This is why we find highly empathic individuals resonating most with practices of shamanism and natural Witchcraft, or with compassion-focused spiritual paths like Buddhism, Hinduism, and mystical arts focused on healing, feeling, and cosmic surrender.

When it comes for the empath to approach magickal work, it's not enough to simply realize that we are experiencing emotions while in the process of meditation or spellcasting – we have to *own* those feelings on a deep level. It's imperative for us Witchy types to follow our trains of thought and observe how our emotions take shape. When a strong emotion arises, it's our duty to fully connect with that part of ourselves. The emotions we are feeling (or aren't feeling) will dictate the direction in which our magickal intention weaves into the tapestry of life. The emotional impact on intent is something that requires perceptive alignment for an effective outcome. Because prayer, spellcraft, and magick are meant to be precise, we must have precision in our emotional awareness.

As we more accurately become aware of our emotional responses and their influence in our lives, we can actively choose which kinds of emotions give shape to our magickal work and to our daily perspectives. When we intentionally invoke empathy for others and for ourselves, the magickal work we perform becomes more reverent and less "needy" because it's in greater harmony with the flow of life itself.

Approaching the Divine

The Divine permeates all beings and truly all things in existence. Both modern quantum physics and ancient metaphysics understand that reality itself is upheld, at least in part, by vibrational essence. Everything has a different frequency, physical and nonphysical, and in the atomic sense, nothing is ever really touching. This is similar to the Buddhist understanding of emptiness: that nothing exists in and of itself, as well as the Buddhist understanding of impermanence: everything is in a constant state of change.

Whereas atheists may purport that nothing in life is sacred or spiritual, the equal-opposite and perhaps paradoxical flipside of this belief is that literally everything in life is spiritually alive. This recognition relates to animism: the earliest human spiritual belief, from which all Indigenous cultures derive – as do all of the world's religions by extension. Animism is the recognition that all things in life, both animate and inanimate, possess spiritual properties and carry either a soul or life-force energy.

When we empaths approach the Divine in any of its forms, we must be selective and discerning. This includes life itself: the grandest ritual of them all. When considering invisible and astral intelligences, however, it's essential that we are informed about the spirit, entity, or energy with whom we seek to interact. We are easily influenced and resonate best with external energies that feel comfortable and safe, including our fellow humans.

We are given the opportunity to judge the extent to which we engage with external spiritual intelligences. We may find ourselves devoted to certain gods or spirits for life, while others are more suitable to respectfully approach here and there, as needed.

This list suggests ways that we, as magickal empaths, can interact with a variety of spiritual forces as we see fit. There are no requirements to the extent to which we work with such forces. Ultimately, it's up to us to determine how our spirit interacts with any given force, and to decide the extent to which we engage with spiritual entities and energies.

- **Ancestors**: Numerous cultures understand that ancestral spirits are consistently around us, often assisting at various points in our lives. This includes departed family, friends, pets, and ancestral spirits of Native lands. For those who work in African diasporic religions, this includes the Orisha, the Lwa, and other ancient ancestors depending on one's cultural persuasion. We can empathetically honor our ancestors through conversation, offerings, regular prayers of gratitude, and by listening to those sudden, fleeting moments of intuition – we never know who may be lending a helping hand.

- **Angels**: Many varieties and hierarchies of angelic spirits are recognized across cultures. Magickal traditions tend to favor archangels ("chief" angels, according to Abrahamic traditions), and many practitioners align with their energies regularly. As empaths, we should research any given angel's history and attributes, and tap into those particular vibrations when working with them. This helps align us to their energies when calling them forth with reverence and honor. Angelic beings respond favorably if they understand they are both respected and empathically recognized rather than trying to be placed in an ideological box.
- **Astrological Forces**: Astrological forces, whether lunar, solar, zodiacal, or planetary, are entities of their own. Although often aligned with gods and goddesses, they remain distinct. We can determine who and what to work with depending on our own empathetic proclivities. Please note that in my book *The Everyday Empath*, also available in Spanish and audiobook, I examine how empaths in particular can interact with both zodiacal and planetary influences at any given time.
- **Cosmic Entities**: A controversial subject, many people believe in humans' ability to contact galactic entities, star beings, extraterrestrials, and other cosmic forces. Whether actual or merely psychological, the empath working with these forces finds the greatest success in extending emotional energy and cosmic love when inviting communication with such forces, whether it be through meditation, channeling, automatic writing, or another form of transmission.

- **Elemental Forces**: Empaths can best connect with the elements through gratitude and contemplation. We can focus on all elements or one in particular, as well as their elemental rulers (sylphs, gnomes, salamanders, and undines, for example), depending on what we're attempting and how intuition guides us. Whichever we're seeking to align with, altering consciousness is key. The rhythm of nature is different from our own. For example, we may find ourselves moving and thinking faster when communing with Fire, or coming to a place of contemplative stillness when working with Earth. By altering ourselves to be in sync with their pace, we are very much empathizing with their own characteristics.
- **Faery Realm**: An ideal empathetic approach to the faery realm is to simply leave offerings of appeasement when intuition guides such. Some ol' standbys are sugar, honey, cream, sweets, ribbons, shiny things, flowers, incense, and miniature houses. Faeries come in all varieties, as I'm certain that European readers of this book are keenly aware, so we must use discernment – for example, try not to barter with them or make a deal. Honoring them is the safest course of action. When working with the fae, go to a natural environment where you can feel their presence. Gently channel your own emotions into their world, abandoning your own insecurities and sense of time. In order for communion to occur, you must try to see how they see and feel how they feel, whisper words of adoration, and lovingly gift your offerings – but always come back to yourself, lest ye be spirited away!
- **Ghosts**: Every culture has a different interpretation of ghosts. If working with personal ancestors, empathy can easily be extended to those we knew and loved, or perhaps have only heard tales about. For spirits we are unfamiliar

with, we need to be on guard. Earthbound disincarnates are individual spirits who still, at least partially, interact with the earth plane. Empaths should be guarded against deception when having ghostly experiences with those whom we are unfamiliar. A good technique is to tap into their energy when you sense them, and then step back to analyze. Empaths are prone to spiritual deception and even walk-ins by ghosts, and must be both highly cautious and analytical (this is mental or cerebral) when interacting with unknown disincarnates.

- **Gods & Goddesses**: When we work with any given deity, we should be as well-informed as possible. Research, both academic and metaphysical, is an essential prerequisite for working with a god or goddess in any regard. By understanding their mythological stories and cultural significance, our empathy can be extended to meet them on their level, offerings and all. In my book *Esoteric Empathy*, I present a sizable list of gods, goddesses, and gender-nonconforming deities that are ideal for empaths to work with.
- **Gurus & Masters**: Some cultures and traditions believe that a very select number of humans attain enlightenment and divine embodiment. Although any given tradition views gurus and masters differently, some of which are in human form and others who are "ascended," we can best approach these elevated beings with humility and open hearts. There are, of course, certain dangers when it comes to individuals who believe themselves – and only themselves – to be God or the embodiment of particular divine beings or forces, which can lead to cultism and blind surrender. Traditions and practices that revere gurus and masters are all different, and we, as wise empaths, need to keep in mind that we are vulnerable to manipulation. At the same time, if we find ourselves

resonating with teachings and traditions of those who are highly revered, whether in the flesh or disembodied, we can choose to empathize and grow from select teachings while simultaneously exercising discernment.

- **Mythological Beings**: Some magickal practitioners enjoy working with mighty beasts of myth and legend. Some say this type of work is the product of fantasy, while others report deeply spiritual experiences. Even if certain mighty beings are the product of human creation, that doesn't make them any less real. Entities of innumerable varieties exist as *egregores* or thoughtforms on the astral plane(s). If an empath chooses to work with mythological beings, their histories and legends should first be astutely researched and explored. We need to exercise caution, realizing that their realities are distinct from our own, even if they can overlap for a time within ritualistic settings. We must preserve our humanness when honoring and gaining the favor of those whose realities are much different from our own.
- **Power Animals**: Indigenous cultures throughout time and culture venerate animals in a multitude of ways. Spirit animals, totem animals, and other terms can be applied to animal manifestations depending on culture, and we need to be careful about appropriation. If the empath feels bonded with a certain animal or animals, we, in general, are connecting with that animal's *oversoul* or overarching energy. We can empathetically connect to animal energy by learning their incarnate habits and tendencies alongside their mythological associations. Through meditation and ecstatic techniques, we can bond with their energies, extending our hearts to dance with their immense power. However one chooses to work with animal guides and helpers, it's essential that we approach their energy how we learn it to be rather than how we

may idealize it. When working with animal energy, we should also exercise awareness in daily choices such as our diets, clothing, and purchases.

- **Spirit Guides**: For many, spirit guides are ancestral spirits here to watch over us for a time. Many metaphysical practitioners also report beings who are "assigned" to a person, and presumably to multiple others, who help nudge us in the correct direction in daily life. Everyone works differently with spirit guides. Personally, I get goosebumps ("chicken skin," as they say in Hawaii) when spirit guides are affirming my intuition, such as during a Tarot reading. Others perceive them in dreams and waking visions, while others hear, smell, or sense spirit guides; these are various manifestations of psychic power or ESP working through our physical senses. However you perceive spirit guides, if you regularly extend empathic gratitude for their presence, they are likely to respond by way of intuitive messages and assistance in your magickal work.
- **Universal Energy**: It truly is profound that we consistently, regularly, and *always* have access to universal energy. Not only are we dancing the dance of life socially, but we are spiraling through space on this incredible sphere that sustains and evolves life itself. One doesn't need to be a Reiki practitioner to access universal life-force. Seasoned Witches and magickal practitioners have their own methods of tapping into certain frequencies, deities, and powers. Generally speaking, however, the same life-force contained within us is all around us, ever accessible from above, below, within, and without. Consider ways by which you can tap into the All, the One, and the Light of life itself. When empathically drained or compromised, use your magick to access the limitless light of universal energy to expand your energy, your magickal practices,

and to assist in any situation. Allow yourself to glow and shine on while inspiring others toward the same.

Approaching Spellcraft

Hop online and you'll find countless spells for cursing someone into ill health, for manipulating people's freewill, for making someone's cattle barren, for causing explosive diarrhea – the list goes on. We empaths are not exactly prone to "black magick," a term I use loosely, because it's not in our nature to intentionally cause harm. When we add a component of self-awareness and emotional humility, practitioners of magick who are *spiritually progressive* can bypass karmic messes by empathically empowering our rituals. By humbly utilizing empathy, we can actively control our thoughts and can invoke a higher level of magickal experience whose energy is more karmically advanced – and thereby more deeply spiritual.

Empathy is a force that helps the world positively change, evolve, adapt, and enjoy the shared gift of life on earth. We support each other. Second only to spells and magickal workings aimed at our personal balance and wellness, an empath's strongest magickal work is *service.* When we consider spellcraft and magickal workings aimed to help make the world a better place in some way, beginning with ourselves, we attune to an empathetic current of evolutionary progression.

As self-aware empaths, when we approach magickal work and spellcraft, we should be fully assured that our workings are designed for the progression and betterment of oneself and others. If a spell or magickal working feels like it's "swimming upstream," or is overly focused on achieving one's desires (personal gain) regardless of consequence, it's not something to pursue. Disharmonious magick throws life off-kilter. Operating esoterically in a manner that is counter to the evolutionary *flow* of reality only serves to disempower all involved.

Our magick should be, to the best of our awareness, performed as an act of service to oneself and life's greater picture. This is the mark of successful and progressive empathetic magick.

What follows is a list of common spellcasting intentions. Empathy can uniquely apply to each intention, strengthening and clarifying our connection to the energy at hand. In the course of our regular magickal practice, we can extend our own emotions into the situation we are aiming to influence. We can utilize empathy toward another person's emotions, toward our *own* emotions, or simply toward a certain *energy*, all of which can serve to strengthen our magickal work and keep it karmically pure.

You will find, throughout each magickal intention, a theme of energetic linking. Empaths should extend emotional energy to any given intention in order to better ensure its success. Unless a spell or magickal operation calls for emotional distancing – a ceremonial procedure methodically invoking precise energies or entities, for example – an empath's personal spellcraft comes to life with emotional investment.

Feel free to utilize these suggestions in your own magickal work and add to the list based on your own reflections and experiences. This is not a list of *spells*, but is rather a list of *suggestions* regarding how a magickal empath can approach any given spiritual intention. This list is designed to serve as an empathetic point of reference to incorporate with your personal spellcraft, ritual, prayer, meditation, and creative visualization.

- **Clarity, Personal**: The empathic key to invoking personal clarity first requires an objective view of what's cluttered. Bring your attention to the unclear situation at hand, empathizing with the manner in which you are perceiving the situation. *Accept* your feelings of struggle or confusion as natural and normal. After you've sat with this energy for a while, skillfully invite clarity into your sphere through any esoteric methods you deem appropriate. (Planetary association: Sun)

- **Cleansing & Healing**: Whether working for yourself or others, begin by emotionally merging with the scenarios you are working with. For example, if you are energetically cleansing a house, open yourself emotionally as you enter each room so that you can accurately perceive which areas need to be cleansed. You are likely to receive intuitive impressions while doing so. Where do you find "pockets" of residual emotional energy? If you are performing cleansing or healing work for another person, briefly merge your consciousness with that individual's chakras, auric layers, and so on, in order to see which work should ensue (in addition to the advice of a physician as needed). Be sure to step back into your *own* energetic body after performing an empathic assessment. Additionally exercise empathy by affirming your client's feelings and by providing emotional understanding alongside a healthy dose of optimistic encouragement. (Planetary association: Jupiter)
- **Communication**: First, forgive yourself and any missteps you feel that you've taken in the course of communication. Extend this empathy to the other person or persons, stepping into their shoes and trying to consider the root of difficulty in communication. As part of your magickal work, vow to "see through the eyes of the other" in the course of any given conversation. If, instead, your magickal work concerning communication is more "generally speaking" – preparing for a lecture or written endeavor, for example – practice invoking compassion, courage, and reassurance focused on your talented self. (Planetary association: Mercury)

- **Cursing**: Cursing is a tricky one because it's usually the last thing an empath wants to do. However, it does have its time and place and should be undertaken with extreme contemplation into whether or not it's objectively for the greater good. In order for curses to be successful, the practitioner must make a concerted effort to emotionally connect with the other person's emotional body. Empathizing with the perspective and plight of the other allows one to step into their consciousness and influence accordingly. Defensive magick, for example, is not amoral; it propels empathy in the long run. This can also allow the practitioner to reconsider the curse before acting on impulse. Also, keep in mind that a temporary binding spell, or a giant "light of awareness" blast is more benign and is often a better option. I examine this "enlightenment blast" alternative to cursing quite thoroughly in my book *A Witch's Shadow Magick Compendium*. (Planetary association: Mars)
- **Death Magick**: Using a representation of death and dying, emotionally connect with the overarching energy of death through deep meditation, reflection, stillness, and the slowing of your breath. Both sorrowful and beautiful at once, Death is the subtle plane of existence just behind Life. Emotionally opening ourselves to this gentle energy connects us to the hidden realms and helps enrich our own perspectives on life. (Planetary association: Saturn)
- **Divination**: Divination should be objective. For this reason, it is wise to *not* overly empathize with a querent (client), but to instead extend your emotional awareness to the spirits you are employing to assist with the divinatory work. After concluding divinatory work for a querent, empathetically open yourself to help them process anything that may have come up in the reading. During the reading, however, stay focused on what you

receive rather than becoming accidentally emotionally swayed throughout the reading. (Planetary association: Moon)

- **Emotional Magick**: When facing difficult emotions, empathy allows the practitioner to feel and accept the sensations that are being worked with. A bit of compassionate understanding goes a long way when faced with darker emotions like anger, shame, and sadness. When something is truly and deeply *felt*, it can allow the door of alchemical transformation to occur. Without the step of empathetic connection, emotionally charged magickal work falls incomplete. For the empath, magick directly concerning emotional work should be undertaken with the goal of emotional alchemy and healthy processing. (Planetary association: Moon)
- **Employment**: Emotionally step into the occupational situation you are seeking to manifest. Feel the emotions created within this job, *not* the details of the job (this can limit your intention). Sit in this energy as long as possible, pulling it toward you with joy. Invite this feeling to recur whenever you think about vocational work of any kind. (Planetary association: Earth)
- **Friendship**: If working to rekindle a friendship, take time to understand the other person's motivations and perspectives. If inviting new friendship, feel the emotional qualities you seek in the other person while you perform sympathetic magick aimed at attracting this individual. (Planetary association: Venus)
- **Global Workings**: Of special relevance to empaths, working magick on a global scale is close to our hearts because we care about everyone and everything, no matter who or where they are. When we are overwhelmed by natural disasters, crime, and political corruption, we can take time to meditatively step into the emotional

energy of a given situation, and help transmute those energies to something lighter, both within ourselves and projected outward to those in turmoil. Make use of white candles, deep breathing, and light-focused visualization. Conduct emotional heaviness through your body (into the left side of your body and projected out through the right), alchemizing heaviness into light. Do not hold onto the emotional weight, because the empath's job is one of transmutation. While empty "thoughts and prayers" only go so far, our *direct* empathetic magickal actions should not be underestimated. (Planetary association: Earth)

- **Grief**: Grief can be a confusing and unpredictable process – but it is a process, and you can help your own processing by ritualizing the emotions. In a sacred space, allow the feelings to come as they do, channeling tears and crying into an object you'll ceremonially destroy afterward. You may wish to collect tears and snot, and then ritually destroy or release them to aid in a manner that aids in your emotional processing. Follow-up your post-grief moments by invoking cosmic energies of peace, comfort, and hope in and around your person. (Planetary association: Saturn)
- **Happiness & Inspiration**: To begin the process of invoking happiness and inspiration, the empath should feel, accept, and channel their own darker (antithetical) emotions. Then, think back to times where you felt completely happy, secure, inspired, creative, and at ease with life. Next, forget about the details and simply sit with that emotion of personal fulfillment. Allow this positivity to fill and fulfill the entirety of your being. Reinvoke this uplifting emotional energy when you are feeling down, discouraged, or pessimistic. (Planetary association: Sun)
- **Health & Healing**: (see "Cleansing & Healing")

- **Hex-Breaking**: If you're feeling safe and confident, place your emotional awareness "into" the curse or hex that may have been cast on yourself or your client. Try to objectively feel its intention. But *do not stop there* or it becomes a dangerous situation. Use your magick to ground the curse into an inanimate object that you will bury, burn, or sink, or you can use a mirror to "return to sender." If you can first *safely* feel the intention that may have been cast, you can then take control of that energy and conduct it accordingly. (Planetary association: Jupiter)
- **Love**: Undoubtedly the strongest force in the Universe, love can be invoked by first loving yourself. The process of self-directed compassion can be difficult in practice but should be applied daily. During those times that you feel content and confident with who you are, use magnetic magick to attract that same force from others in the world. Practiced regularly, it may be surprising to see the ways in which the vibration of love manifests itself. (Planetary association: Venus)
- **Memory & Study**: When you are working to commit something to memory, utilize your emotions to forge a link with the information itself. Whether you're studying a period in history, a meticulous math problem, or a foreign language, get creative to draw some kind of emotional association with the details you're studying. We are likely to have better memorization abilities if we can associate minor emotional responses with cognitive information. (Planetary association: Mercury)
- **Prosperity & Luck**: Being a complicated subject linked to our survival, magick revolving around prosperity requires that we spend time emotionally disconnecting from ideas of "worth." Reconsider idealizations you

may have about both poverty and wealth. Aim to replace feelings of desperation with feelings of spiritual trust. Emotionally feel your worthiness *and* your ability to be financially responsible while you invoke energetic prosperity. Tap into overarching energies of abundance and draw that emotional fulfillment toward you as a daily routine. (Planetary association: Jupiter)

- **Protection**: Emotionally merge into the *need* you have to create protection. It doesn't matter what is being protected: yourself, a client, a pet, a house, a situation, and so on. The most important aspect of this magick is to feel the need and trust yourself while you craft the intention. (Planetary association: Mars)
- **Sleep & Dreaming**: When working magick aimed at sleep or the realm of dreams, it's essential to make your thoughts "fuzzy." By calming the rational mind and letting the creative side take hold, one begins to step into the terrain of the unconscious. Empathically, you may extend your emotions to the experience of sleeping itself, or may merge your thoughts with what it feels like to astrally project, experience prophetic dreams, or whatever the goal may be. Feel the emotional fulfillment that comes from rejuvenating the body throughout the night. (Planetary association: Moon)
- **Spirit Work**: Whether you're working with ghosts, deities, guides, or guardians, take some time to emotionally merge with their realm and sidestep your own fleeting emotions. Once you have empathized with their spiritual essence, step back into yourself and respectfully perform your work and communication. (Planetary association varies)
- **Travel**: Empathically connect with your "future self" while you perform magick associated with travel. See yourself happy, content, and safe at your destination.

Draw an energetic link by feeling those emotions yourself in the present moment. Regularly reinforce the visualization before and during the course of travel. (Planetary association: Mercury)

- **Weather Magick**: Whether praying for rain or otherwise seeking to influence weather patterns for the greater good, take time to focus and step into the results you seek. Visualize deeply and strongly, witnessing atmospheric currents changing form. Communicate with these forces, telling them why you're attempting to help direct their fluctuations. Feel your energy and intention merge with the desired intention, and be sure to properly honor the mighty forces you're approaching by gifting offerings and prayers. Weather magick generally requires repetitive practice to reinforce the intention. (Planetary association: Earth)

Empathic Energy Maintenance

Empaths are very sensitive to energy fluctuations throughout the day, as well as within dreams; we just can't escape it! We understand that life is a constantly evolving, never-ending process of change; no moment is the same as the last, at least from our limited human perspectives. Where does our empathic energy fit in to all this? We often struggle to understand where our energy is expended or unnecessarily drained.

Highly empathic souls are often unaware of where and when we "drop" energy in daily life, sometimes accidentally allowing small things to affect us to a degree more than necessary. Even the smallest exchanges can sit in our field of energy, building invisible momentum, eventually spilling forth with tears and confusion. The more committed we are to self-awareness, the more keenly we can observe our own emotional and energetic fluctuations in daily life. This is part of bringing our magick to life.

Throughout the day, we may pick up on others' emotions, for better or worse, and not realize that they have affected us. An example I can cite about this is when I was recently told by a family member that another family member's beloved dog had crossed the rainbow bridge that morning. The family member I was talking with was upset, but not extraordinarily sad. I texted condolences to those who lost their pup, and went about my day. That evening, having forgotten about the exchange, I found myself deeply sad. I was contemplating the loss of my cats from the past, and was overcome with anxiety about the inevitable passing of my own familiar, Catskills. Prayers ensued to Bast (Bastet), and it was only later that I remembered the earlier exchange about the dog. I had clearly held onto the exchange on a subtle level, somewhere beneath my conscious radar, and was affected without knowing why.

Because empaths are prone to holding onto energies, we must exercise as much genuine self-awareness and mindfulness as possible throughout the daily cycle. This also brings about the need for frequent breaks. Whether it's lying down for ten minutes or going to the bathroom to splash water on the face, it's wise for us to take brief moments of realignment, and to engage in proactive daily practice. This looks different for everyone.

Daily Practice

Daily practice begins with nightly practice, and you've heard it all before: try to fall asleep and wake up at the same or similar time every cycle, avoid stimulants and screens close to bedtime, don't have too much alcohol in the evening, meditate whenever possible, and so on.

Proper sleep is important for highly sensitive souls, especially those of us who are inherently connected to unseen planes. Even if we forget the details of our dreams, our unconscious minds have gone through the motions and are affected by dreamtime's general energy. Dreaming often involves processing difficult emotions, so if we wake up off-kilter, it can throw off our whole day. We can start our daily practice by reflecting on our dreams. Dream journals are excellent ideas, or we can simply sit in meditation and bring to mind what we remember, even if it's just the general energy of the dreams. From there, stretch your arms real big, draw down cosmic energy, and surround those images and feelings with light. This is part of setting your energy for the day.

As morning goes on, and as time allows, be steadfast with your daily practice. It doesn't have to be much, especially at first, but as with anything, once you get in a rhythm and cycle, daily devotions will become effortless.

Yoga in its physical form (*asanas*) is very much a type of meditation, not merely a workout. Listen to your body and stretch to get the blood flowing and the energy moving, even if it's not yoga on a mat, and even if the movements are entirely intuitive. Focus on the breath, and consider learning breathing exercises.

Stretch, shower, brush teeth, use the bathroom, shave, grab coffee, and whatever is your normal routine, but be sure to integrate some amount of spiritual practice, even briefly. Only you can determine what sets you right for the day. For some, it's extended yoga practice, for others it's prayers to their guides, gods, and guardians, and for others it's getting outside to soak up the sun and feel the elements directly. If performing a proper ritual, like the LBRP (Lesser Banishing Ritual of the Pentagram) sets you right in the morning, go for it! Do what works best for you so that you can face the day with awareness and courage.

If you're inclined toward astrology or esoteric Qabalah, consider daily practices that are aligned to the day's planetary hours or astrological configurations (there are some great apps for those), or simply to the ruling planet of each day according to classical astrology:

Sunday: Sun
Monday: Moon
Tuesday: Mars
Wednesday: Mercury
Thursday: Jupiter
Friday: Venus
Saturday: Saturn

As the day winds down, especially during that liminal time of dusk, chemical changes take place in the brain that allow us to go within and self-examine. Look back on the day and see where extra energy may have been placed, willingly or unawares. If you find yourself at a good energy level, it's likely that you maintained your personal energy that day. If you're feeling drained, take some time to reflect on what happened throughout the day. Were there exchanges or experiences, even brief, where you could have deposited extra personal energy? If so, visualize those times and send them light while simultaneously pulling back a cord of energy. Visualization goes a long way, and is naturally tied to magickal work.

If scanning your energetic body in the evening, you may notice imbalances or excessive energy in one or more chakras. See this book's Opening Meditation for brief information on each chakra. Perform realignment techniques to your own discretion, not negating cleansing your aura and physical body if necessary.

If needed, perform some intentional energetic dumping to refresh yourself in the evening. The simplest way is to take a shower and scrub yourself with sea salt. Or, take a bath with herbs, oils, and salts. You may choose to burn sage, incense, and cleansing herbs while meditating, or may create an evening prayer routine to honor your deities, ancestors, or invisible protectors. It's worth experimenting to see how you can realign your energy after having gone about your regular day. And don't forget the rejuvenating power of naps!

The Importance of Grounding

Because empaths can so easily be swept away by emotional experience, we must remain anchored at all costs. We can't be social all the time, nor is it healthy to become hermits or shut-ins. There's always a balance, and we are responsible for finding it.

Anchoring items can be of benefit, such as a special necklace or keeping grounding stones in the pockets. Even tattoos and body art can serve as spiritual anchors and reminders to stay in our bodies and within our own healthy emotional spheres. Naturally, grounding meditations, such as the common tree-rooting visualization, can be helpful alongside deep, slow breathing techniques and *pranayama*.

Let it not be understated that simply walking or standing barefoot on Mother Nature herself, whether grass or dirt, stones or sand, creates an instant electromagnetic link to the earth below: an opportunity for instant grounding. Some studies suggest that this link is most strongly forged by connecting barefoot for at least thirty minutes.

The dance of energy around us can be disorienting at times. We need to ground in the body so we don't get lost in our emotions, which can lead to escapism, delusion, and flights of fancy. Escapism avoids our karmic responsibilities.

It's essential that we not ignore our bodies. If the body needs some exercise, make it happen! If the body wants to rest, take some downtime without shame. If the body is hungry, grab a little snack, and if you need to use the bathroom, don't put it off. These responses are an act of grounding because it assures the body, and therefore the unconscious mind, that it is safe and doesn't need to enter anxiety mode. The body slowly becomes more stressed as its needs are not met, so if we're able to tend to our bodies like we would a pet or child, we are then practicing multilevel self-regulation.

The word *somatic* refers to physical sensations in the body, and how our nervous systems respond. This is why we find therapists encouraging patients to feel "where" an emotional sensation is located in the body. Like an observer, we can comfort that part of the body through touch, kind words, and deep breathing. This is part of self-care because it helps reassure the safety of the body and mind. We might not always realize how our bodies are neurologically reacting to thoughts and stimuli, but we can catch and comfort ourselves to assist in grounding. Somatics are hands-on self-comforting and healing techniques that go beyond mere cognitive understanding. I encourage readers to research somatic techniques and nervous system regulation, as these gentle-yet-effective methods of mind-body awareness are keys to grounding in daily life, most especially for those of us prone to regular episodes of anxiety.

Part of grounding is getting out in nature. We are Pagans, after all! It can be connecting and rejuvenating to do something as simple as a hike, or standing outdoors to feel the presence of animals and the elements. One can connect with the elements even more deeply by building a fire, swimming in a river, rock climbing, or skydiving. The elements are here for us to honor and enjoy, and by working with them regularly we also balance the elemental forces within ourselves.

It's good to pay attention to the weather, as each one can have different effects on the mind and body. Empaths are sensitive to weather conditions, and they tend to have a direct impact on our mood, even if we don't realize it in the moment. Daily weather patterns also provide an opportunity to more deeply connect with Mother Nature and with ourselves. Here are some examples:

- **Sunny**: Summon the purifying light of the sun to cast away mental and emotional debris. Perform calls to solar deities, meditating on the sun's role in the sustenance of all life on Earth. Call forth the Oak King and other archetypes of life, fertility, and vitality if it's your practice.
- **Snowy**: Make prayers, calls, and offerings to Jack Frost: the archetypal Holly King of the bitter season. Lay in the snow, put energy into snowballs, and meditate on your deeper nature: snow draws one's energy into oneself and aids in purification. Snowy environments allow for reflection and contemplation to occur quite easily if we have a place of safety and shelter nearby.
- **Rainy**: Like sacred tears, utilize the releasing and unburdening power of rain. Surrender to the element of Water, dance in the raindrops, and let the water wash

away pain and difficulty in your life. Perform heavy workings with Water and its associated spirits. If rainfall evokes sorrowful energies within you, use the pouring rain to help purify these feelings, alchemizing them into emotional nourishment.

- **Foggy**: Because fog represents mystery, utilize its eldritch energy to pierce "through the veil." This is particularly significant during heavy fog, when the point before us can barely be seen with the naked eye. This makes the deeper planes more accessible, and allows one's outdoor magickal work to be naturally shrouded.
- **Hailing**: Hail can be seen as representing anger: ice falling from the sky. Allow the hail to invigorate you, charge you, and get your magickal juices flowing. Dance in the hail, allow it to sting your flesh; these are kisses and scourges. Contemplate how you have suffered in your life in order to learn. The hail will melt and alchemize, much like the harsh emotions we've experienced in the past.
- **Storming**: Storms are pure, raw energy. The storm is a grand purging, and a palpable reminder of nature's intensity. Utilize the storm to raise extreme energies of any type. Cast your spells with force, shout the sacred names, and merge your own energy with the glory of the storm.
- **Overcast**: Gray days… they draw us inward and force us to be reflective. Use overcast days for highly personal, transformative magick. These are the ideal days to meditate, chant mantras, relax in the bathtub, or turn the pages of an occult tome. This is also a great time to create art of any kind, and to offer prayers of gratitude.

Magickal Empathic Techniques

We empaths should regularly utilize techniques of energy processing, lest we become overtaken by emotional excess. Emotional energy, most especially for us, needs to be properly conducted in order to uphold a healthy self.

As many occult systems profess, energy enters the left side of the body and exits the right. Remember the phrase *left: receive, right: release*. Although I cannot entirely speak on behalf of those who are left-handed, who were unusually repressed by Christianity in the West for years (because the left hand is the devil hand, of course), the energy of life still enters on the left and exits on the right as a general rule. This is an excellent point of knowledge when conducting spells and magickal rituals. It's also essential to know when functioning in life.

When casting magickal energy in an intentional spell or ritualistic procedure, mind that energy enters on the left side of the body. When projecting energy outward, do so with your right hand, or the right side of your body. Many Eastern spiritual systems value the right side of the body for a reason. It is generative and progressive, which is a reason to always give offerings to gods and spirits with the right hand, regardless of religion or culture.

Throughout your day, notice how you can conduct energy that enters your sphere. Empaths are transmuters of emotional energy, plain and simple. When emotional energy gets stuck in our bodies we become depressed, apathetic, and sick. It takes an acute daily awareness to conduct the energy around us. We are conduits!

Catch yourself. This is hard for empaths. Catch yourself in any given moment and observe the conduction of emotional energy in your sphere. Because we are accustomed to living in the moment, it may feel unnatural to take a breath and step back to observe the energies at hand. To maintain wellness, we should briefly and regularly step back and bring focus to the mind in order to observe. Doing so is integral for our spiritual health and survival. Our lives are an interplay of mindful objectiveness and emotional involvement.

The reality of life on earth is that it contains an astounding amount of suffering, chaos, and grief. A common response to this is based in fear, causing a person to become bitter, nihilistic, misanthropic, or self-serving. The more enlightened response, based in love, is that of empathy: the knowledge that we are all suffering together, and we deserve to lift each other up and create a positive impact while we are here. Even if it's dreadfully difficult, even if we're prone to pessimism, and even if we wake up dreading another day, there is a reason we are here and there is something we can offer.

The work of a magickal empath takes place on a daily basis, and is mainly found in social interaction. We don't have to be constantly on top of our game, but we can choose to be genuinely positive and helpful to the best of our abilities at any given time. We can do this without depleting our own energy; life is all about finding balance. We must work to meet our own needs on all levels to be able to gift others with wellness.

Naturally, self-care comes first and is an ongoing process, but caring for oneself and caring for others are not mutually exclusive. Empaths gain a sense of fulfillment when helping others in need, whether human, animal, or environmental. There are countless ways we can put this into action, much of which I cover within my book *Esoteric Empathy*.

Consider volunteer opportunities, such as with homeless shelters or animal shelters. If you have the funds, research reputable organizations whose causes you can get behind – just ensure that their staffing structure allows the majority of funds to be put to proactive use, not just line management's pockets. We are here to make a difference and this can be done in innumerable ways. This also filters to our daily choices, purchases, and interactions with others. Even when we are struggling, we can be a positive force in the world.

Protection & Projection

Empaths are in need of energetic protection but simultaneously struggle to maintain it. For the most sensitive among us, even the smallest emotional exchange can throw us off-kilter, making it feel like our protective efforts are all for naught. However, if we are regularly practicing protective techniques, these boundaries and shields can be reconstructed very quickly. The trick is to not allow our minds to convince us that our protective efforts have failed or that our shields have been shattered.

Once we have constructed energetic shields, their imprints remain around our bodies and are accessible even if something "gets through." Once we recognize ourselves as having been emotionally swayed, whether by someone around us, by reading the news, or anything else, we can take a moment to remember our shields, quickly visualize them, and notice that they reconstruct themselves quite effortlessly.

The goal is not to shut out every emotion around us; that would be going against our nature. We *do* want to interact with reality. An empath's shield should allow for good stuff to get in and bad stuff to keep out. This is why our most effective shielding tends to be the visualization of spheres astrally "composed" of crystal, elemental energy, or universal light. There are countless ways to visualize shields, and each person should find what is the most effective for them. Additionally, you may find it most effective to perform shielding when hopping out of the shower in the morning, or perhaps upon completing morning stretches and prayers.

We can call upon the elements, the archangels, our guides, and other helpers to assist with shielding. We can integrate stones, herbs, incense, and other tools if we feel the need. The most effective empathic shielding is something reinforced on a daily basis, although many empaths prefer to increase the level of protective force shortly before venturing into a public or social situation.

It's wise to integrate a short affirmation when visualizing protective shields. You can come up with something short and sweet to remember, such as, "I am now protected and safe; only love can enter my space," and recite it every morning when prepping for the day. If you feel your shields are compromised at any point throughout the day, take a moment to breathe, visualize, and silently recite your affirmation. The process of reconstructing shields is remarkably quick, and relies on your attentiveness to emotional and energetic fluctuations.

A great number of metaphysical empaths find that shielding and grounding exercises, whether brief or ceremonial, are complementary and best performed together.

When it comes to daily interaction, be aware of eye contact. Being windows to the soul, a great amount of energy is exchanged through eye contact, emotional and otherwise. As with anything, find a balance. If you're overwhelmed, a little less eye contact would be wise. Instead, look at someone right between the eyebrows when conversing; one can't tell the difference.

If you're feeling anxious, measures can be taken for blocking your own third eye. Hats, caps, wigs, bindis, and other accessories can go a long way in acting as covert magickal shielding items. If you're feeling bold but need protection, I've discovered that using prosthetic glue to adhere a small mirror (the kind from a craft store) to the brow does wonders – but only in context, like going out to a nightclub or festive event.

The clothing, accessories, and colors you wear also influence the emotional energy we might receive in any given situation. Consider the crowd, and modify your appearance for the occasion. Use your intuition to determine how public interplays of energy might occur based on how you appear to others. Energy can be unconsciously deposited by others with even a glance, so be prepared for social occasions of any type. Ideally, you'll gracefully dance any given experience and will have protective methods in place preemptively. It's not that being social is dangerous, but that we, as magickal empaths, should be prepared for whatever might come our way – life is unpredictable.

If it feels like you're absorbing too much emotional energy from others in public, don't be shy about taking a little space to collect yourself. Empaths tend to be people-pleasers, often giving in to social expectations in an effort to not rock the boat. However, part of defining our needs is politely taking space to ground and center when needed. Even a walk around the block, a "smoke break," or going to the restroom can suffice, depending on the situation. If someone judges you for taking a breather, who cares?

Strong empaths are introverts, even if we have extroverted moments from time to time. Allowing for personal space, especially when we can even briefly surround ourselves with nature, is an act of self-care and sometimes self-preservation. Magickal empaths are especially "different" from most others, so some of our needs will be different from the norm. We can respect and honor ourselves by taking personal space when needed.

Boundaries are a matter of self-respect. Boundaries are not something that one places on another person, but are rather the definitions we place on ourselves to protect our wellness. Boundaries refer to what we choose to engage in versus that which we choose to disengage from. Unhealthy boundaries, however, can stem from trauma or harsh experiences in the past. Boundaries can be rational or based in fear. Whether healthy or fear-based, boundaries communicate our needs in life.

Social boundaries have to do with our own responses; not dictating others' actions. If someone behaves in a way that creates discomfort, for example, our boundary is to respond by stating that we will disengage if the behavior continues. Establishing boundaries has nothing to do with commanding another person to act in a specific manner, but rather is about setting limitations regarding our own lives.

Boundaries can be tough for empaths because of that innate "need to please," as we don't want to cause disturbance. We are excellent at avoiding conflict, but not the best at defining ourselves. But it's not impossible; everything takes practice.

It's wise to become aware of the sensation of discomfort. When you feel it rise within yourself, consider ways in which you can respond that honor your needs first and foremost, whether it's taking a break to think, or entirely disengaging from a situation. Remember, you are an adult and are not obligated to fulfill everyone else's desires; you can leave any situation at any time.

I am not saying to become entirely soft, because there are some situations and social exchanges worth fighting for. Establishing your space is paramount when it comes to boundaries, which directly ties in to empathetic protection. Other situations, such as when you know you can't change another person's harsh mentality no matter how hard you try, require separation. Over time, the developed empath learns the difference, and realizes that it's not rude to separate or define oneself during challenging social exchanges; it's a matter of self-preservation. We deserve peace, wellness, and the same level of respect we extend toward others.

Empaths are conductors of emotional energy, both our own and that of others. We can easily become overwhelmed with emotional energy from outsiders, which can serve to create personal despair, addiction, isolation, and a slew of other negative responses. However, that's not what we're here to do. We are here to make a positive difference.

It's vital to keep in mind that empaths are not pathetic emotional sponges. There is a lot more to us than that! In fact, we ourselves are constantly influencing our environment, subtly affecting the emotions of those around us, on a constant basis. This is especially the case when interacting with other folks who are also emotionally or psychically sensitive. Our actions, reactions, and interactions have an influence on others' experiences and therefore our own in return.

We normally consider the empathic experience to be something absorptive, considering it comes naturally to us to step into other people's worlds of emotional experience. But that's only half the picture. It may seem that we only absorb surrounding vibes, but there's another side to the empathic coin: *projection*.

Empaths are capable of transmuting energy instantaneously. For an empath to enter a balanced state, which by all means waxes and wanes depending on the day, we need to remember that we are helping conduct the rhythm and flow of our lives on a constant basis. We aren't only influenced; we are influencers.

Subtle and unseen energies (and for us, particularly that of the emotional variety) enter through the left side of the body and are conducted from the right, as I mentioned earlier. This process of absorption and projection is noted by numerous esoteric schools of thought. If you become aware of your personal aura and body's energy right now, at this moment, you may note that sensations seem to enter the left side of your body and expel on the right. This is part of life's dance.

Aside from my own writing, particularly in my book *Esoteric Empathy*, I haven't witnessed other empathic specialists discussing the reality of what I term "projective empathy." This refers to our ability to project emotional energy into our reality; particularly emotional energy that we have internally transformed, having previously absorbed. This relates to magickal protection because we are not required to *carry* the emotions of those around us.

It's simple: visualize emotional energy entering the left side of your body and exiting the right in a lighter state. By conducting and transmuting emotional energy into a lighter state, we aid those around us while remaining balanced ourselves. This balancing act can happen on a consistent basis, whether it's during normal social operations – which includes social media and virtual outreach – or whether it's during a time of difficulty. This is a fast visualization and magickal operation that can occur either in a ritualistic setting or covertly during the course of everyday conversation.

When you are interacting with someone who is in a state of grief, anger, mania, or another overwhelming state, it's possible to empathize with them without holding onto their emotional experience. Absorption occurs instantly for strong empaths, which is why we need to be prepared for anything. We can choose to feel, but not attach to, another person's intense emotional energy by instantly conducting the absorption out of our body's right side, visualizing the energy transformed into light and comfort. This fast conduction of emotional energy allows for *sympathy* to occur in the moment without an overload of empathic absorption.

Conducting challenging emotional energy into a higher frequency is one of the most incredible gifts of the empath. Still, if you find yourself overwhelmed and spiraling in a challenging social exchange, take space: it's not selfish, it's wise. If you find yourself in a dangerous social situation, remove yourself. Social discernment takes time and practice, and it begins by putting yourself first by necessity.

Another avenue of empathetic transmutation and projection is the creative process. We empaths find beauty and curiosity in even the smallest things, which makes us natural artists. In addition to learning how you personally conduct emotional energy during social exchanges, you should never disregard your nature as an artist; an interpreter of life. Part of the process of conducting energies around us is to express them in some manner, and sometimes this can best take the form of creating expressive works. One of the most beautiful things about being empathic is that our creative work comes with a unique wallop of emotional impact.

I find myself at my artistic best either when I'm writing or when I'm building up to a personal spell or ritual. In the past, I led and hosted Pagan and Hindu ceremonies for a great number of individuals, and I found this to be an excellent creative outlet. In the even further past, I used to create Gothic photographic art, and before that I was intent on creating poetry and the occasional sketch or painting. Way, way before that, I used to play dress-up with friends and also performed in childhood plays at a local theatre.

A big reason why I've been personally able to maintain some level of emotional equilibrium is due to always having a creative outlet. We all have natural creative proclivities, so determine some of your own unique callings and pursue them! You are a magickal empath, and there is great work to be expressed. Things don't have to be perfect, but don't sell yourself short: you truly are an innate artist. Regardless of creative medium, and putting aside a desire to impress other people, you have energies that need to be conducted and transmuted by way of creative expression. Pursue and indulge your inherent artistic gifts, whatever they are, because that's part of our life's process.

Water & the Moon

The magick of empathy is naturally aligned to both the moon and the Water element. We understand that the ocean is connected with lunar tides, and both of these physical and mystical aspects go hand-in-hand. In modern occultism, the Water element became tied with the cardinal direction West by the Hermetic Order of the Golden Dawn, who were looking in particular to ancient Greek associations for the four directions.

When it comes to Water and the Western quadrant, we see that the sun descends in the West. This connects us to mysteries of shadow; things that often go unseen (like emotion), reaffirming our abilities of emotional conductors and magicians of shadow. In Wiccan and Neopagan systems, the Western quadrant is aligned with energies of release, processing, feeling, and, of course, empathy.

Empathic magick should follow the lunar cycles. Emotional energy is both subtle and profound, making the empathic mysteries aligned directly with Lady Luna. The manner by which we perceive her cycles from Earth are of great significance to the magickal empath. Although we celebrate and revere the solar Sabbats, we find ourselves most at home with the lunar Esbats and the turning of the lunar tide.

The more we track and attune with the moon's cycles, the better we come to know ourselves as magickal empaths. We have learned the basics – the full moon is a time for spellcasting, the new moon is a time for rebirth and shadow work, the waxing is for increasing something, and the waning is for banishing – but we should also consider zodiacal influences at any given time.

The full moon always occurs in the opposing zodiac sign as the Sun is in, while the new moon occurs in the sun's same sign. We can balance our magick accordingly. While I will not go into detail about astrology here and now, as I explore in detail both zodiacal and planetary influences in my book *The Everyday*

Empath. We can use our learned wisdom alongside that from other sources to investigate any given lunar fluctuations at play. We can time our emotional magick and general awareness in conjunction with the lunar tides and the ever-changing zodiacal configuration to more deeply attune to subtle energies that are at play, influencing us oftentimes at degrees we're not aware of.

Coming back to the subject of the Water element, there are numerous ways by which we magickal empaths can attune to the element and enjoy its profoundly healing, cleansing, and rejuvenating properties. The following list gives suggestions for tapping into Water in a variety of metaphysical manners. The Witchy or magickal empath can most easily find balance and empowerment when aligning with the element in one form or another.

- **Asperging**: To asperge an area is to sprinkle the space with water, much like we see in traditional Wicca as part of the casting of a circle. Often performed with enchanted saltwater or another type of holy water, the elemental energy enters the space or person getting blessed, and the protective vibrations continue as the water droplets slowly evaporate.
- **Baths**: We empaths love our warm baths. Relaxing and calming, bathing centers our energies, cleansing our bodies and minds. Bathing is one of the most effective methods of empathically cleansing and emotionally resetting. Spruce up your bath with magickal potions, herbal sachets, sacred salts, gemstones, and an atmosphere aimed at harnessing your intention.
- **Blood Magick:** A watery elixir from our body itself containing our very own DNA blueprint, a drop of blood can be used in any magickal work that is deeply personal and relevant to our innermost selves. Consider pricking a finger to add a bit of blood on candles, papers of spiritual

petition, or to bind an item to you personally, such as Tarot cards or divinatory tools. Be cautious when utilizing blood magick, not only because it requires penetration of the skin (aside from menstrual blood, used for releasing), but because the direct energetic link should be yours to utilize, and yours alone. Using one's blood in magick is very personal and should be kept that way with cautious awareness.

- **Float Tanks**: Float tanks, being watery isolation chambers, are excellent empathic tools. The float tank experience is offered in many cities, and allows the empath to enter a state of deep meditation in a dark setting. Sensory deprivation allows us to truly be with ourselves. The suspension in Epsom saltwater induces a unique feeling of timelessness that's beneficial for inner work and spiritual rejuvenation.
- **Floor Washes**: Popular in hoodoo and related systems, mopping a floor with the addition of a magickal component serves to introduce an intended energy that permeates one's whole living quarters. Floor washes are readily available in magickal stores and online, and one can also find instructions on creating their own by searching the internet.
- **Hydration**: It's easy to forget to drink our water throughout the day, but it's vitally important. Lubricating the body from the inside out, pure, fresh, clean drinking water helps every level of the self from cell to spirit. Bottled water often contains loads of microplastics, so source your water in the most mindful way possible in your environment and give thanks for its purity, as many others in the world are not afforded the same luxury.
- **Mars Water**: Although rarely needed, a good magickal tool for the empath to keep on hand is Mars Water. Because rust is related to the planet's warring, protective

energy, one can create this magickal component by soaking genuine iron nails in water until the mixture turns a shade of rust. This water can be used in any magick aimed at protecting against influences that wish to cause harm. Be cautious when using this, as merely touching the water can cause anger, aggression, and harshness to arise in the practitioner.

- **Moon Water:** It is a fun and rewarding activity to create Moon Water. While there are no strict definitions in doing so, I might suggest the following: place a piece of moonstone in a clear glass jar filled with the most pure, natural water you can find. Put the jar outside for three nights: the night before the official full moon, the full moon eve itself, and the night thereafter. Enchant the water each of those nights by energetically "linking" the moon to the bottle. This water can be used as holy water for empathic blessings and cleansings, asperging for purification, and to bless both altars and magickal tools.
- **Potions & Elixirs:** Whether brewed in a cauldron or bubbled on the stovetop, potions can contain any magickal ingredient under the sun. Not generally designed for drinking, potions can be used to bless an area of land or be creatively integrated in spells aligned to the intention at hand. Unless strained and frozen or otherwise preserved, potions have a short shelf-life and should be used in magick relatively quickly upon creation. Some potions, however, are designed for consumption and should be preserved accordingly.
- **Showers:** Showering is an act of cleansing the body, mind, and spirit. Whether taken in the morning to wake up or later in the day to refresh, it's helpful to visualize the shower's water flushing any negativity from the crown through the body, out the feet, and down the drain. It is wise to chant mantras, affirmations, and gratitude

when showering off. Every act of showering can be one of refreshment, rejuvenation, and total cleansing.

- **Swimming:** It's a freeing experience to take a swim. Activating the body's inner fire through movement, the watery immersion balances the exercise in a unique manner. Although public pools can be great, swimming in a natural body of water is especially cleansing for empathic souls. If one's energetic need is more subtle, simply soaking in a lake, hot spring, or the sea can invite emotional healing and refreshment by way of watery meditation.
- **Teas & Beverages:** Tea, coffee, and other drinks can be enchanted with intention, most especially intentions linked to properties the Water element and/or the esoteric properties of the steeped herb. Wine, beer, and spirits can also be enchanted, but should be approached with caution, if at all. Alcohol of any type carries energies of the Fire element and should only be consumed mindfully due to its insidiously altering effects on the mind, body, and emotional state.
- **Witch Bottles:** Called an *apotropaic* charm, meaning one that guards against malicious influence, Witch bottles are profoundly protective magickal tools used in ancient and modern times. These are magickal shields that confuses and traps negative energy being sent in one's direction, intentionally or unintentionally. Simply procure a glass jar and fill it with multiple sharp objects from nails to broken glass. Fill the jar with your own morning urine when completing the spell (hence the Water association), and place it either somewhere hidden near your home's entrance or indoors where it can't be found. Regularly direct external harmful energies to the bottle, and be sure to throw it away if you move.

Keep in mind that empaths are particularly prone to falling too deeply into the Water element and its attributes. When it feels like we are emotionally drowning, we need to take a step back and analyze ourselves from a mindful perspective. Look for remedies.

One of the best ways we can do this is by mentally cataloging different experiences in life to see where they fall on the spectrum of the four terrestrial elements. The "element" of Spirit (Akasha, Quintessence) permeates all four elements rather than merely being distinct, and any elemental experience can be "spiritualized." For example, putting magickal energy into food preparation, which is related to the Earth element, instantly transforms something mundane into something sacred.

If we are "in too deep" with the Water element, the following symptoms may emerge:

> Depression, frequent crying, spacing out, *ennui*, becoming over-reliant on divination, overusing alcohol, overusing sedating drugs (such as opiates, benzodiazepines, or dissociatives), frequent oversleeping, isolation or withdrawal, excessive daydreaming or "spacing out," a preoccupation with thoughts of death, and so on.

Here are some activities to help the overwhelmed empath balance out a bit in terms of elemental connection. I recommend any of the following activities that call to you, alongside the standard recommendations of emotionally processing through therapy, journaling, medical assistance, and meditation.

> **Earth**: Gardening, getting out in nature, camping, cooking fun new recipes, tending to pets and animals, working with herbs, planning ahead, volunteer work, sewing and crochet, horticulture, canning, sculpting, old world skills, and so on.

Air: Reading, studying, creative writing, exploring incenses and scents, making music, exploring astrology or traditional sciences, handwriting letters and postcards, organizing your schedule, painting or sketching, journaling, socializing with good friends, and so on.

Fire: Dancing, exercising, traveling, exploring your sexuality, decluttering your home, cleaning and cleansing, performance art, dressing up, candle making, hot yoga, attending local events, taking up new activities, and so on.

Tools for a Magickal Empath

There exist quite a few natural tools that we can put to use as magickal empaths. Nature holds answers and medicines for what ails us. For empaths, protection, confidence, and emotional healing are our primary areas of focus.

This list briefly describes the *most* empathically-relevant natural tools at our disposal that we can utilize for assisting in daily functioning. Their magickal usages come from a variety of times and cultures, and although we don't have time here to dissect their specific origins, it's valuable to know that these and other tools are available, accessible, and readily usable in daily life and in spellcraft. Follow your intuition when determining how and when to use any given item, whether it's in a formal ritual or in everyday life.

Whenever possible, buy your materials (especially gemstones) from suppliers who explicitly state that their items are humanely sourced and gentle on the environment. It's our duty as Pagans to be as aware as possible about the process of supply and demand, and there is no harm in asking suppliers about their sources if we feel the need, be it gemstones, food products, herbs, or anything else.

- **Black Tourmaline:** Renowned as the most protective stone for an empath, black tourmaline can be worn, carried, or used in magick to establish energetic boundaries. Many empaths wear the stone in large public settings, reporting its effectiveness in blocking excessive external vibrations. I advise against wearing or carrying the stone daily, as we don't want to become energetically isolated, and to rather utilize it occasionally as needed.
- **Citrine:** The stone citrine is yellow and radiant, and is said to have no energetically absorptive qualities as a result. Its energy is one of self-confidence and illumination, and is particularly helpful to wear or carry when the empath is engaged in an activity that requires a joyful boost of strength.
- **Eggshells:** Eggshells, as well as discarded nests, are profoundly protective tools for empaths. Considering the shell's protective symbolism, we can integrate eggshells in magick to protect our emotional energies and disallow too much influence from outside sources. Hoodoo makes use of *cascarilla,* utilizing powdered eggshell in small paper cups that are placed at the corners of a room, bed, or home. These cups can also be used as magickal chalk when inscribing sacred symbols on pavement. Ground or powdered eggshell can be used in protective magickal work in countless ways, so follow intuition and give thanks to the animals that contributed to the work at hand.
- **Fossils:** Fossils of any type, including petrified wood, connect us with deep, ancient energy, and are perfect for carrying on person or utilizing in magick aimed at grounding and centering. Fossils serve as a link to the past, and are excellent to have on hand when performing past life regression, shamanic soul retrieval, and any type of work aimed at healing trauma.

- **Mirrors:** Handheld mirrors can be used in magickal work to deflect and reflect unwanted emotional energies. One can draw symbols on craft mirrors using paint or permanent marker, helping protect the practitioner from empathic overload. Keep in mind that we are emotionally deep ourselves, and often need to process emotional energy through our own systems. Other times, protective tools like mirrors can guard against excess from the outside.
- **Moonstone:** Because the moon is connected to the oceanic tides, its energy is aligned with the Water element, which is also the element associated with the empathic experience. When performing magick aligned with cycles of the moon, utilizing moonstone in any regard aids the empath in spiritual alignment.
- **Obsidian:** The deep black color of the stone obsidian hints at its properties of protection against overwhelming vibes and, in our case, emotional overload. Wearing the stone, carrying it, or utilizing it in protective magick has great benefit for highly empathic souls. Because it is prone to absorbing external energies, be sure to regularly cleanse and purify any pieces that are utilized.
- **Rue:** An herb widely utilized in hoodoo and associated traditions, rue is used for guarding against energetic excess, aiding in the cleansing and purification process. This is particularly relevant to empaths who have "picked up" too much external emotional energy along the way. One of the most common uses is to put it in a sachet that can either be carried or soaked in the bathtub for the purpose of emotional protection, cleansing, and coming back to center.
- **Salt:** Any form of salt, whether mineral salt, sea salt, Himalayan salt, or black Witch's salt, is a tool of instant shielding. In addition to helping create ramparts of protection, salt is used as a purifier, especially when

mixed with water, and can help the empath both purify and protect at the same time.

- **Yarrow:** Yarrow is known for carrying numerous magickal properties, one of which is defining boundaries. The herb can be steeped as a tea, sprinkled around oneself in ritual, grown on one's property, or utilized in the form of a tincture or flower essence. Empaths can tap into yarrow's properties of energetic protection and guarding against emotional drainage.

Entering the Magickal Flow

We all know the phrase "getting in the flow." The phrase has an encouraging tone; one lacking stress and boosting confidence. As opposed to *going with* the flow, which tends to be passive, *getting in* the flow implies action and involvement. When it comes to magickal work and spiritual work, this is a must: we must be in a deeper creative flow than usual in order to create, manifest, and project our intentions into reality.

Empaths are sensitive to the world at large, and are often acutely aware of things that go under most people's radars. (To be fair, we are also sometimes oblivious to things that are *on* everyone else's radar, but I digress.) We experience reality from a heightened state of emotional awareness and perceptibility.

As spiritual artists, we co-create and build our experiences of reality through intentional magickal work and by way of our daily thoughts and actions. Spiritual rituals of all varieties, including life itself, primarily rely on the practitioner.

Our attitudes and approaches are the most important components to our work. Regardless of how many sigils we draw, regardless of how many deities we call forth, and regardless of how rare the ingredients are that we use in a spell, the success of our work depends primarily on *ourselves* as the crafters: the architects.

We cannot force creativity, art, or magick. As I presently write these words, I feel a certain confidence and creative spirit. I am in the flow. For that reason, these words come easily (but they wouldn't necessarily have done so yesterday, for example). It flows; it's not forced. The words write themselves, in part, and I am merely a conduit or co-creator. The same holds true for other works of art and for works of magick.

The illustrious, revolutionary, and ever-controversial occultist, Aleister Crowley, once said that all magick is art. As all artists know, art cannot be forced; the same goes for magickal work! We can try to force it, and sometimes successfully so – but the most successful and least stressful method of creation is to get in the flow to see where and how we are taken.

"Flow-states" occur when we feel aligned, balanced, and confident. This makes a huge difference in our intentional work and in our lives in general. But it's not always easy to get to this place. There are times when life sucks, or at least appears to suck. Life can be dreadfully stressful, amazingly beautiful, and everything in between. Even when we are sad or stressed, we can count on life to pick us back up and align us once again with that spiral flow: a feeling that assures us that everything is somehow in its proper place. From this mental, emotional, and spiritual state, we can intuitively feel that everything is happening for a reason and that we are exactly where we are supposed to be. From this place, a sense of trust, compassion, and spiritual connectedness has a chance to develop and flourish.

Everyone has a baseline personality, and this baseline can change with time. It's a noble goal to work for both personal happiness and for the happiness of others. If, however, you feel that your baseline personality is attached to ongoing fear, anxiety, sorrow, and pain, or if you experience extreme highs coupled by extreme lows, I encourage you with all my heart to seek counseling, therapy, and/or medication from a mental health provider. Life is much too short to live in a perpetual state of darkness, and we *all* deserve the healing it takes to reach a general baseline of happiness in life, or contentment at the very least.

Our responses to life's challenges are what define our energetic state. If we live in a constant state of stress, agitation, or depression, we are certainly not in the flow. And while it's rare that a person can remain in a perpetual state of confident bliss, everyone has moments of "okayness" and universal connectedness to varying degrees. These are the moments we can most especially engage with life in a creative and magickal sense.

The brain is an intricate piece of equipment, processing both subtle and complex information at speeds incomparable to even to the world's greatest supercomputer. Our minds are capable of feats we may never fully understand. Metaphysical practitioners recognize not only the mind's connection to physical senses, but to the psychic world, the spirit world, the dream world, to past lives, and to genetic memory. The list is endless, and we find our perceptions continually returning to the eternal moment of *now*.

As I mentioned earlier in this book, we magickal empaths must learn to train our minds. Our thought processes are intricately linked to our emotions. Both of these things are linked to our past experiences. As we react to life's various experiences, it's essential to examine the reasons behind our responses. What is the basis for our mood at any given moment? The more frequently we choose to step back from our thoughts and emotions, the more clearly we can view ourselves. The more frequently we can simply *observe* life without dramatically emotionalizing even the smallest things, the deeper we grow in self-awareness. Self-awareness and mindfulness help us get in the groove of positivity, lending immeasurable strength to our magickal lives, our empathic skills, and our uniquely individual works at hand.

Pagan, Wiccan, and otherwise Witchy readers are likely familiar with Starhawk's classic *The Spiral Dance*. Affirmed in this groundbreaking book is the fact that everything in life is consistently in flux. Nature's spiral dance is reflected in the cycle of the sun, the moon, the planets, and the cycle of birth, life, death, and rebirth. We dance the spiral of life in everything from hunting to ceremony to social interaction to the moments between breath. All around us and within us is life's spiral dance. Dancing the spiral can be considered a core of our Craft.

When we are a state of flow, we are vibing with life. Moreover, we are *dancing* with life much like India's Lord Shiva (Siva/Mahadeva) in his aspect of Nataraj (Nataraja), depicted in a state of endless cosmic dance. We see Lord Nataraj as an emblem of the perfect Lord of the Dance. Like all Vedic gods, goddesses, and devas, Shiva Nataraj is portrayed in a manner that is rich with symbolism in order to both convey the deity's qualities and to provide a focal point for devotees.

Nataraj is portrayed within a burning ring of fire (*Agni*) and also holds a lick of flame in his left hand; this symbolizes the god's alignment to life's nature of change, often termed "destruction." However, Nataraj stands atop a lotus pedestal, representing life's perpetual experience of rebirth. Directly under his right foot we see him "taming" or overcoming what is often called "the demon of ignorance." A snake (*Naga*) coils his waist (representing *Shakti* or *Kundalini* power). He wears the clothing of an ascetic or sadhu, signifying the power of renouncing worldly attachments. He is pictured holding a *damaru* drum to represent the constant rhythm of life. His hands and feet are depicted in significant postures and *mudras*, and the holy river Ganges flows outward from his dreadlocked hair.

Shiva is regarded as the ideal Yogi, Swami, and *Brahmachari* (renunciant). In his avatar of Nataraj, he is the perfect spiral dancer who is entirely in the flow of evolution and awareness. In this aspect, Nataraj is not preoccupied, is not distracted, and is not anything but present. By performing his *dharma* (or "will," as a Thelemite might say), Shiva Nataraj is very much "in the flow" of life and existence. We can call upon Shiva and other blissfully enlightened deities in order to help ourselves remain in the flow of life, determinately devoted to equilibrium. The combination of "love" and "flow-state" is of particular resonance to highly empathic souls; indeed, these forces are both healing and aligning.

Speaking of Eastern mysticism, after having worked alongside Timothy Leary and his LSD experiments at Harvard University in the 60s, psychologist Ram Dass went on to take a disciplined Hindu path under the auspices of Indian guru Neem Karoli Baba. His most celebrated piece of work is the immeasurably creative art-book *Be Here Now*. In addition to this monumental piece of work and a number of other books, transcripts of a 1970 lecture at the Menninger Foundation in Kansas were published in a book called *The Only Dance There Is*. Gracing an early edition of the book's cover, naturally, is the beautiful Shiva Natraj. Within the lecture, Ram Dass lovingly conveys,

> *Everything you do, whether you're cooking food or doing therapy or being a student or being a lover, you are only doing your own being, you're only manifesting how evolved a consciousness you are. That's what you're doing with another human being. That's the only dance there is!*

He goes on to examine different social roles we humans "play" from one scene to the next in life's great cinematic experience. From a place of expanded awareness, life itself is more like a play in which we can simultaneously be the actors *and* the audience. From one contextual moment to the next, we dance life's spiral to and fro. When we are aligned to a higher frequency, this dance becomes something fulfilling and sacred, while the flipside to this can be called a downward spiral, which can lead to a Dark Night of the Soul, as coined by sixteenth-century mystic St. John of the Cross, as well as to self-harm and self-destruction. The experience of a Dark Night is meant to break us down and build us back up into something beautiful; it is an emotionally alchemical process of "out with the old, in with the new."

Through conscious effort, mindfulness, and present-moment awareness, we can avoid downward spirals by centering in the eternal *now*, and by performing shadow work on a regular basis. (This process looks a bit different for everyone.) For highly empathetic individuals, maintaining a state of emotional balance is of utmost importance in life's unfolding adventure.

We've all been there: pouring laboriously through loads of books and websites to search for the right ingredients, incantations, or symbols to use for a spell. There's nothing wrong with research. However, it's essential to methodically craft our magick. The entire process of piecing together information and writing a spell or ritual becomes nearly effortless when we are in a state of flow, dancing with the rhythm of life. Rather than frustratingly pouring over research, our intuition will guide us to the resources we need. When we are in the flow, we will know which websites to click on, which symbols or words to use, and in which books to check indexes.

When we are actively experiencing a flow-state, we will know which herbs to add, subtract, or substitute during spellwork, for example, and we find that our intuition (and perhaps our spirit guides and guardians) easily communicates components and procedures of spells or rituals. When we are in the flow, we know what to do, where to look, and how to accomplish our magickal or creative goals, whether for ourselves or for others.

Again, we cannot force healing, creativity, or magickal prowess. When a flow-state vibrational alignment occurs, the magick simply creates itself and we become inspired toward self-improvement.

When aligned with the flow, we can more easily see the greater picture of any given situation, and can be of much better assistance as a result. Whether it's Witchcraft, ceremonial magick, hands-on healing, prayer, yoga, meditation, or artistic work of any kind, everything makes sense and comes easily when we are in the flow with life's infinite dance.

Magickal work, and indeed the magick of itself, relies on the choices we make in any given moment. If we are connected to the present moment, aware of the nature of infinity, and feel a sense of confidence, we can tap into the projective force of evolution propelling all energies forward in space and time. When we dance with life's progressive metaphysical flow, our magick and our art becomes crystal clear; we know what to do and how to do it within our unique realms of knowledge and capability. From this space, we are riding the progressive wave of conscious evolution. When there is magickal or spiritual work to accomplish, we can witness a high level of progressive success from a state of flow. We become empowered and confident as magickal empaths when we are dancing in unison with the all-pervasive energy of life's nonstop evolutionary process, and it's that state of frequent spiritual alignment we should all strive for on a regular basis.

We must love and value ourselves irrevocably, and must do the work to forgive our mistakes and move on from life's most difficult times. We must, every day, do our best to remember just how deeply important we are in the world. I'm glad we exist.

Dance with joy, live with love, and always be blessed.

Closing Meditation: Working with the Shadow Self

The experience of life requires both resilience and humility. Possessing high levels of empathy requires that we have strength and confidence throughout our earthbound adventures. We cannot buckle to sorrow or overwhelm. To become aware of our internal strength is to gain the responsibility of healing our wounds and lifting up others while we are here.

We have all made mistakes and missteps. We have all been touched by life's traumas, dramas, and painful experiences. But these things do not define us. We are our own worst critics, and it's easy to hold onto pain and mistakes we've experienced, but we absolutely must move onward. Our true essence is goodness, and the echoes we create in life are our magick. We must strive to make a positive impact, both daily and in general. If we don't do it perfectly, that's okay! We just need to do our best.

To actively embody our strongest and most empowered attributes, we have the responsibility of working with our shadows, with our egos, and with our personalities. This work begins internally, is an ongoing process, and takes a hefty amount of honesty. The better we know ourselves, the mightier the impact we have in helping make the world a better place as empowered, magickal empaths.

If you are interested in more deeply exploring the energy of "shadow" as it applies to oneself and the greater world, I humbly refer you to my expansive book *A Witch's Shadow Magick Compendium,* which I wrote with empaths and sensitive souls in mind.

The following is a meditation which is designed to access challenges associated with internal darkness. This "darkness" contains repressed fears, uncomfortable memories, and subconscious habits, many of which influence our everyday lives. These are essential to navigate for personal development. Mystical and magickal practice help us learn about, and work with, our shadows.

This meditation is one step in the process. Please read through it a number of times before enacting so that you are able to perform it by memory. Alternatively, make a recording of yourself reading it calmly and slowly, utilizing appropriate time gaps, as to guide yourself working through the exercise.

1. Situate yourself in sacred space where you can relax in comfort. Perform this meditation in dimness; the liminal time of dusk is preferable. A new moon is most auspicious. Cast a circle in your usual way. Ignite a black or green candle, fire up some all-natural purifying incense, and settle in. Summon the elements. If you are working with relevant "shadow-friendly" deities or spirits, call upon them now with reverence in a way you see fit. Do your thing.
2. When you feel connected and aligned, recline and declare your intent. Say something like, *"Behold! Great spirits of obscurity and memory, I now enter the shadow of my mind. Darkness is my teacher. I embrace my shadow as a force of creation and mystery. Sacred spirits of the inner planes, I humbly ask that you guard and guide me into myself, that I may grow and learn with patience and accuracy."*
3. With your eyes closed and your body comfortable, visualize the room around you. Allow your mind's eye to focus on the room from your perspective, feeling the placement of the environment. While performing visualization, practice deep and slow breathing. Continue to alter your consciousness and become more keenly sensitive. Take a decent amount of time to expand your perception. You are safe.

4. Now sufficiently aware, envision your astral body descending through the floor, a few feet into the earth. You are comforted by sensations of peace and stillness in this place. Open your psychic senses and feel the burrowing creatures and worms. Feel the roots of trees, plants, and mycelium brushing your body. Feel the damp soil, recognizing it as a center of nourishment and creation.
5. Knowing that you are protected by the bounty of the living earth, bring to mind two or three occurrences in your life that caused you sufficient amounts of pain and emotional suffering. Take some time to remember these occurrences; some may pop in your mind immediately, while others may be shrouded and even willingly repressed. If you happen to recall an overload of painful experiences, you may wish to write these down after the meditation so that you can perform this again with different focuses in mind. Monitor your mental health and take it at your pace. You are focusing on the most traumatic, painful, and emotionally-breaking experiences you have endured in your life. Be courageous, brave, and determined in the face of these. If tears surface during the meditation, allow yourself to cry. Process each experience individually, slowly, remembering these things even if you have already worked through them in the past. Claim your power. (If these memories cause too heavy a disturbance, consider processing them in a therapeutic setting instead, as we are not looking to retraumatize ourselves!)
6. If you're comfortable sifting through harsh experiences of the past, continue by sorting through each occurrence individually. For each one, take plenty of time to recall the specifics of each situation: how did you feel at the time? What was your role in the situation? How has the situation effected your personal development? How has

it impacted your life? Are any of your current patterns of behavior connected to the event? Can you forgive yourself for mistakes, and can you release the energies of others involved in the occurrences? How can you work with these challenges, and how can you allow them to remain in the past?

7. When you run through each event in your mind, you should feel a return of emotional weight. Envision your astral body still submerged in earth – covered with a dense, black energy. This represents the extent to which your mind still holds onto the occurrence; the extent to which it plagues you now. When ready, visualize a soft, healing green-colored light emerging from your heart center, radiating through your body, and eventually to the dense astral matter surrounding your frame. Envision this light conquering the etheric junk, permeating through it and conquering the pain, the shame, the astral weight. Breathe. With a strong exhalation, envision the black substance breaking away from your aura, plummeting down into the earth as an offering. Envision the healing light surrounding your astral frame, guarding against its return.
8. Once you have performed this with each individual occurrence in mind, visualize your astral body rising up from the earth, through the floor, and back into your physical frame. Wiggle your fingers and toes, breathe deeply, and come to center.
9. To close, state your intention, saying something like, *"Sacred spirits here this night, I thank you for protecting and comforting me as I journeyed layers of my mind. I ask that I be able to understand and release these issues by continuing to face them bravely and accurately. Thank you for attending this ritual of transformation."*

10. Take some time to come back to your body, and close the circle as you normally would. It's good to write down your experiences afterward, and spend additional time meditating on the intricacies of each experience. Repeat this when you feel called to do so, and don't feel as though you need to overcome absolutely everything from your past in one sitting. Everything in life, no matter how dark and painful, can hold profound lessons beneath the surface, and can help us develop in the most extraordinary ways as the beautiful, magickal empaths we are. Be blessed, be confident, and be empowered! So mote it be.

Bibliography & Suggested Reading

Aron, Elaine N. *The Highly Sensitive Person: How to Thrive When the World Overwhelms You*. Secaucus, NJ: Birch Lane Press, 1996

Belanger, Michelle. *The Psychic Energy Codex: Awaking Your Subtle Senses*. San Francisco, CA: Weiser, 2007

Bennett-Coleman, Tara. *Emotional Alchemy: How the Mind can Heal the Heart*. New York, NY: Harmony Books, 2001

Bohart, Arthur C. & Greenberg, Leslie S. (Editors). *Empathy Reconsidered: New Directions in Psychotherapy*. Washington, DC: American Psychological Association, 1997

Coyle, T. Thorn. *Kissing the Limitless: Deep Magic and the Great Work of Transforming Yourself and the World*. San Francisco, CA: Weiser, 2009

Crowley, Aleister. *777 and Other Qabalistic Writings*. Boston, MA: Weiser, 1986

——————. *Magick, Book Four: Parts I-IV*. Boston, MA: Weiser, 2004

Ekman, Paul. *Emotions Revealed: Recognizing Faces & Feelings to Improve Communication & Emotional Life*. New York, NY: Holt, 2003

Cunningham, Scott. *Cunningham's Encyclopedia of Crystal, Gem & Metal Magic*. St. Paul, MN: Llewellyn, 2005

——————. *Cunningham's Encyclopedia of Magical Herbs*. St. Paul, MN: Llewellyn, 1984

Dass, Ram. *Be Here Now*. Kingsport, TN: Hanuman Foundation/ Lama Foundation, 1978

——————. *The Only Dance There Is: Talks at the Menninger Foundation, 1970, & Spring Grove Hospital, 1972*. Garden City, NY: Anchor/Doubleday, 1974

Digitalis, Raven. *Esoteric Empathy: A Magickal & Metaphysical Guide to Emotional Sensitivity*. Woodbury, MN: Llewellyn, 2016

——————. *The Empath's Oracle*. Woodbury, MN: Llewellyn, 2022

——————. *The Everyday Empath: Achieve Energetic Balance in Your Life*. Woodbury, MN: Llewellyn, 2018

——————. *A Witch's Shadow Magick Compendium*. Chicago, IL: Crossed Crow Books, 2022

Farrar, Stewart & Janet Farrar. *A Witches' Bible: The Complete Witches' Handbook*. Custer, WA: Phoenix Publishing, 1981

Goldie, Peter (editor). *The Oxford Handbook of Philosophy of Emotion*. New York, NY: Oxford University Press, 2010. (Articles referenced by A.W. Price, Christopher Gill, Peter King, Jesse J. Prinz)

Goleman, Daniel. *Emotional Intelligence: Why it Can Matter More Than IQ*. New York, NY: Bantam Books, 1995

Greer, John Michael. *The New Encyclopedia of the Occult*. St. Paul, MN: Llewellyn, 2003

Harner, Michael. (editor) *Hallucinogens & Shamanism*. New York: Oxford University Press, 1973

Hatfield, Elaine C.; Cacioppo, John T; & Rapson, Richard L. *Emotional Contagion*. New York, NY: Cambridge University Press, 1994

Hay, Louise L. *You Can Heal Your Life*. Carlsbad, CA: Hay House, 1999

Horne, Fiona. *The Art of Witch*. NSW, Australia: Rockpool Publishing, 2019

Iacoboni, Marco. *Mirroring People: The Science of Empathy & How We Connect with Others*. New York, NY: Farrar, Straus & Giroux, 2008

McLaren, Karla. *The Art of Empathy: A Complete Guide to Life's Most Essential Skill*. Boulder, CO: Sounds True, 2013

Melody. *Love is in the Earth: A Kaleidoscope of Crystals*. Richland, WA: Earth-Love Publishing, 1991

Mesich, Kyra. *The Sensitive Person's Survival Guide: An Alternative Health Answer to Emotional Sensitivity & Depression*. Lincoln, NE: iUniverse .com, Inc., 2000

Orloff, Judith. *Emotional Freedom: Liberate Yourself from Negative Emotions & Transform Your Life*. New York, NY: Three Rivers Press, 2010

Sangharakshita. *Know Your Mind: The Psychological Dimension of Ethics in Buddhism*. Birmingham: Windhorse Publications, 1998

Saraswati, Swami Satyadharma; translated by Ruth Perini (Srimukti). Yoga Kundali Upanishad: Theory and Practices for Awakening Kundalini. Independently published, 2019

Silverknife, Zanoni. *Lessons in Georgian Wicca, 101-104*. Class handouts and lecture notes. Missoula, MT, 1999

Starhawk. *The Spiral Dance: A Rebirth of the Ancient Religion of the Great Goddess*. San Francisco, CA: Harper & Row, 1979

Subramuniyaswami, Satguru Sivaya (Gurudeva). *Merging With Siva: Hinduism's Contemporary Metaphysics (The Master Course Trilogy)*. Kapaa, Kauai, HI: Himalayan Academy, 2003

Tolle, Eckhart. *Stillness Speaks*. Novato, CA: Namaste/New World Library, 2003

Yronwode, Catherine. *Hoodoo Herb & Root Magic: A Materia Magica of African-American Conjure*. Forestville, CA: Lucky Mojo Curio Co., 2002

MOON BOOKS

PAGANISM & SHAMANISM

What is Paganism? A religion, a spirituality, an alternative belief system, nature worship? You can fi nd support for all these definitions (and many more) in dictionaries, encyclopaedias, and text books of religion, but subscribe to any one and the truth will evade you. Above all Paganism is a creative pursuit, an encounter with reality, an exploration of meaning and an expression of the soul. Druids, Heathens, Wiccans and others, all contribute their insights and literary riches to the Pagan tradition. Moon Books invites you to begin or to deepen your own encounter, right here, right now.

If you have enjoyed this book, why not tell other readers by posting a review on your preferred book site.

Bestsellers from Moon Books
Pagan Portals Series

The Morrigan
Meeting the Great Queens
Morgan Daimler
Ancient and enigmatic, the Morrigan reaches out to us. On shadowed wings and in raven's call, meet the ancient Irish goddess of war, battle, prophecy, death, sovereignty, and magic.
Paperback: 978-1-78279-833-0 ebook: 978-1-78279-834-7

The Awen Alone
Walking the Path of the Solitary Druid
Joanna van der Hoeven
An introductory guide for the solitary Druid, The Awen Alone will accompany you as you explore, and seek out your own place within the natural world.
Paperback: 978-1-78279-547-6 ebook: 978-1-78279-546-9

Moon Magic
Rachel Patterson
An introduction to working with the phases of the Moon, what they are and how to live in harmony with the lunar year and to utilise all the magical powers it provides.
Paperback: 978-1-78279-281-9 ebook: 978-1-78279-282-6

Hekate
A Devotional
Vivienne Moss
Hekate, Queen of Witches and the Shadow-Lands, haunts the pages of this devotional bringing magic and enchantment into your lives.
Paperback: 978-1-78535-161-7 ebook: 978-1-78535-162-4

Bestsellers from Moon Books

Keeping Her Keys

An Introduction to Hekate's Modern Witchcraft

Cyndi Brannen

Blending Hekate, witchcraft and personal development together to create
a powerful new magickal perspective.

Paperback: 978-1-78904-075-3 ebook 978 1 78904 076 0

Journey to the Dark Goddess

How to Return to Your Soul

Jane Meredith

Discover the powerful secrets of the Dark Goddess and transform your depression, grief and pain into healing and integration.

Paperback: 978-1-84694-677-6 ebook: 978-1-78099-223-5

Shamanic Reiki

Expanded Ways of Working with Universal Life Force Energy

Llyn Roberts, Robert Levy

Shamanism and Reiki are each powerful ways of healing; together, their power multiplies. Shamanic Reiki introduces techniques to help healers and Reiki practitioners tap ancient healing wisdom.

Paperback: 978-1-84694-037-8 ebook: 978-1-84694-650-9

Southern Cunning

Folkloric Witchcraft in the American South

Aaron Oberon

Modern witchcraft with a Southern flair, this book is a journey through the folklore of the American South and a look at the power these stories hold for modern witches.

Paperback: 978-1-78904-196-5 ebook: 978-1-78904-197-2

Readers of ebooks can buy or view any of these bestsellers by clicking on the live link in the title. Most titles are published in paperback and as an ebook. Paperbacks are available in traditional bookshops. Both print and ebook formats are available online.

Find more titles and sign up to our readers' newsletter
http://www.johnhuntpublishing.com/paganism

Follow us on Facebook

https://www.facebook.com/MoonBooks

Follow us on Instagram

https://www.instagram.com/moonbooksCI

Follow us on Twitter

https://twitter.com/MoonBooksCI

Follow us on TikTok

https://www.tiktok.com/@moonbooksCI

What People Are Saying About

Magick for Empaths

This book is insightful, inspirational, and enlightening. It explores numerous aspects of the empathic experience and how it relates to magickal spirituality. This easy-to-read mini-book is a must for all empaths, to dip in and out of when they feel the need to seek inspiration. Raven, thank you for sharing, and for being unashamedly you.
Laura O'Rourke, editor of *Witches Magazine*

For the magician, empathy is more than the ability to understand and share the feelings of another sentient being. What my empath friend Raven Digitalis presents to us with this marvelous little handbook, is a practical guide to applying this most fundamental magical talent – a tool that grows increasingly more powerful as your consciousness, and your LOVE for ALL expands.
Lon Milo DuQuette, author of *The Magick of Aleister Crowley, Low Magick*, and *Enochian Vision Magick*

Groundbreaking, practical, and powerful. I'm thrilled about Raven Digitalis' approach to linking empathy to the magickal, especially with the emphasis of actualizing the compassionate nature of emotional psychism to invite the highest designs for self and the world.
Cyndi Dale, author of *The Subtle Body, Awaken Clairvoyant Energy*, and *The Complete Book of Chakra Healing*

As a priest and celebrant, I find myself stepping into the emotional experience of hundreds of people every week. This book will speak to different people in different ways. For me it is a gift that offers invaluable insight into my own empathic vocation, pointing me to techniques that enable as well as practices that protect.
Mark Townsend, author of *The Gospel of Falling Down* and *Diary of a Heretic*

Raven Digitalis reveals the mystery of being an empath. In *Magick for Empaths,* Raven breaks down what being empathic means and gives us masterfully created techniques to help us delve into our abilities so that we can connect to others for magick and healing. Open your heart and mind and discover where the magick of being an empath can take you.
Chris Allaun, author of *Whispers from the Coven* and *A Guide of Spirits*

This powerful guide is destined to become a classic for those drawn to esoteric healing and the mysteries of magick. In a time when global distress can feel overwhelming, my friend Raven offers us the tools to reclaim our inner power and be the light the world so desperately needs. With profound gratitude, I endorse this essential book for anyone seeking to harness their empathic gifts and transform darkness into healing energy.
Avi Lago (Avinash Lagoo), Witch, Tantrik, Ayurvedic Consultant, Theosophist, and Theosophical Society Librarian